MOVING FORWARD
Walking Out of Bondage Into Freedom

Written by:
Denva Smith

Moving Forward, *Walking Out of Bondage Into Freedom*

Editing and layout by: Ya Ya Ya Creative (yayayacreative@gmail.com)

ISBN No. 978-0-692-38853-2

PRINTED AND BOUND IN THE UNITED STATES OF AMERICA

Acknowledgements

First, I give thanks to God for His goodness and His mercies in my life. I thank Him for giving me the opportunity to write and encourage those who may need it right now, especially those who are broken. Thank you, Lord!

To my children, Tito Jr. (Troy), Teshane, Rayhan (Dhane) and Shayna. I thank God for blessing me with you. Each one of you are special to me and most importantly, to God. None of you were accidents, but were divinely brought to the earth for such a time as this. I love you guys.

To my sister, Claudia, thank you for believing in and supporting me through thick and thin. Briana, thank you for always believing in your Aunt. Much blessings.

To every reader of this book, please remember that there is nothing too hard for God. Commit your ways to the Lord. Trust Him and He will bring to pass whatever it is that you are trusting Him for. Thank you.

Table of Contents

Introduction

After writing, erasing, and re-writing over and over again, I finally understood what the Lord wants me to focus on in this book. His focus is the emotional healing of His wounded daughters, binding up the brokenhearted, and introducing Him as father to the fatherless. In addition, He wants me to encourage women to rise up from the ashes of their broken past and move forward in Him.

In spite of all that has being designed to hold us back or to stop us, we must decide to rise up out of the ashes of our past hurts and pains, and move forward into the great things that God has preordained for us. For many of us, God will challenging us in this season to rise up, let go of yesterday's troubles, for today is a new day. The Lord is doing a new thing and now it shall spring forth.

Behold, I will do a new thing,
Now it shall spring forth; Shall you not know it?
Isaiah 43:19 (NKJV)

In this new thing, God is giving us freedom from whatever has held you and I in bondage. Many of us have been carrying weights and burdens that have held us back. For those who have been on a broken track, God is now taking you off and He is putting you back on the right track so that you can move forward freely. This is the season when we release all past and present negativity and look ahead. This is what the apostle Paul says, "Brothers and sisters, I do not consider myself yet to have taken hold of it. But one thing I do: forgetting what is behind and straining towards what is ahead." (Php 3:13 NIV)

From time to time, some of us may have even find ourselves sidetracked by the memories of our troubled past, however, getting up from where we are and taking small steps will automatically puts us in forward movements. Whatever it is that you have dreamed of accomplishing in your life, now is that time to get up and try. There will be oppositions, criticisms, discouragements, and negative self talks. The opportunity will present itself for you to give up, but do not. Push past all hindrances and move forward.

It is my prayer for you that you will know you are on God's mind and that He loves you. Know also that God wants us whole and fulfilled in every area of our lives and He is going to make it happen; all for His glory!

PART I

CHAPTER 1
Questions for God

Have you ever questioned God's love for you? I have, in times past, and you probably have too. If He really loved me, then why did He allow so much brokenness, such abuse, the abandonment, the losses, and the rejections? You may not find your questions for God in this list, but the fact remains that we have all asked God questions, especially when life does not seem to make sense.

I once heard someone say, "Who dare put a question mark where God puts a period?" In other words, "How dare you ask God any questions! Don't you know that He is God?" While we know and understand that yes, He is God!, it is also accurate to say that God does not mind us asking Him questions. It is important to realize that it is in the questioning that we get clarity and answers for the reason why we struggle.

A few days before writing this chapter, I found myself in questioning mode. I wanted to get some answers from God about my finances. I soon realized that I needed much more than just answers about money, so I went into a seeking mode.

I felt the need to pray until something happened, so that is what I did. I was persistent in prayer about getting answers from God. Because I did not get the answers that I was seeking right away, I continued to seek the Lord. The thought that stood out to my spirit was that no one who seeks the Lord will come away empty.

For example, Jesus shared a parable with His disciples to show them that they should always pray and not give up. He told the story of the judge who neither feared God, nor cared about man. When a certain widow continually cried out to him for justice against her adversaries, he gave it to her, lest she would have worn him out. The Lord then says, "Listen to what the unjust judge says. And will not God bring about justice for His chosen ones, who cry out to Him day and night? Will he keep putting them off?"

The answer is no! When we cry out to God in our distress, our cries will not fall on deaf ears. God is faithful and kind and always wants what is best for us. He is telling in this parable that if we persist in prayer, there is nothing that He will not do for us, so long as it is His will for us.

> *Ask, and it shall be given to you; seek and you will find; knock, and the door will be open to you. For everyone who asks, receives; the one who seeks finds; and to the one who knocks, the door will be opened.*
> Matthew 7:8 (NIV)

At the time, I was out of a job and one of the answers I was looking for was how to get money to pay my bills. That answer did not come at the time, instead in that moment God answered the true cry of my heart. There was always a void in my heart that stemmed from not having a relationship with my natural father. As a result, I did not know how to relate to God as Father either. It is often said that we see God in the same way we see our fathers, and that I have realized to be true.

During this time of seeking the Lord, I noticed that I had somewhat of a longing for something I had never experience with my father. I longed for a close relationship with an earthly dad. I was saying to God, "Lord, I want to experience what a relationship with a father is like." There was a hole in my heart and it was a void that I needed filled by a father. The truth is, that hole was there all along, but God chose to uncover it in that moment so that He could start the healing process.

The Lord had reserved that moment to draw me into dialog with Him. This was a father-daughter moment that was set on the Father's calendar from before the foundation of the world.

As a child, my most vivid recollection of my father was that of someone pointing him out to me as he rode back and forth on the train. As I grew older, I remember seeing him a few more times, but each of those times he was severely drunk.

In the past, the absence of a father in my life did not mean much to me because I could not remember him being a part of my foundation. As I became older, I realized how much that relationship was needed. As the Lord pointed out some of the deep-seated issues that were the result of not experiencing a father's love, I realized how much I was really affected. Knowing that my father had passed away, the only thing I could do was cry out to God to fill that void.

It was mind boggling for me to learned that so many of my struggles were direct results of not having a father figure in my life. For instance, my lack of trust. It was hard for me to trust anyone growing up, with the exception of my sister, Claudia, and a few others. Other than these few, I had not build a trusting relationship with anyone for a long period of time. It is often said, for anyone to trust another, one must first get to know that person. That is something I had not done in the foundational years of my life.

I had self-esteem issues, I felt a sense of worthlessness and disconnection from not having anyone to tell me or show me who I was. Even the deficit in my decision-making abilities was a result of not having that foundation with my father.

THE PROCESS

The word *process* implies a series of actions or gradual changes that leads to a particular result. However, for many of us, the process is not welcome at all. We want to achieve results in one, maybe two steps, but that is not how our loving Father does it. You see, the bad situations that some of us have experienced may not have happened one or even two times, instead, over a period of time. For some, their exposure was during childhood and continued into their teenage years. Others, it has followed them through to adulthood. Can you imagine God uncovering your entire history in one day for you to process? You would probably end up in an asylum! God will not bring something to light that would devastate you. If He brings it to light, then that means it is time for you to deal with it.

The Lord started the healing process in me at the moment I set out to seek Him. Although I thought that He would have healed me at once, He did not. Instead He has been bringing me through a healing process, one step at a time. I am learning things about my Heavenly Father, and myself that I did not recognize before.

Please allow me share this story with you. I recently had the opportunity to sit in prayer / deliverance training at my home church. We were given a worksheet and were asked to describe how we pictured Father God and His activities in our lives. After I read the first question, I was literally stopped in my tracks, due to the image I had of my Heavenly Father. In fact, when I became aware of my actual thought process and of how I really saw God, it blew my mind. It was shameful for me to put on paper that I saw Him as someone sitting on His Golden throne, far, far beyond the blue, in the southwest corner of heaven. In my mind I knew that He was watching, He could hear me, but I could not see much more activity.

I learned that day that the way I viewed Father God was a direct result of how I viewed my earthly father. He was not there for me while he was alive, but had I really tried, I could have gotten in touch with him.

During this process, I learned that my Heavenly Father was closer to me than I thought. He truly loved me and was not somewhere far beyond the blue, only reachable through much effort.

Once I was made aware of His nearness, I wanted to talk to Him more and more, and He talks back to me more and more too. It is not that the Spirit of God was not talking to me all along, instead it was that I had the wrong concept of His commitment and love for me.

Before I go any further, some may be asking, "Does God speak to His people?" The answer to that is yes! He speaks by way of His Spirit–The Holy Spirit. (John 10:27 KJV)

What this process revealed to me was that although we know the Lord and may have a true relationship with Him, we still have mind-set and ideologies that need to be exposed to the light and truth of God's word. God does not always reveal all the hidden things at once, because we could not bear them. He reveals in increments knowing that whatever He reveals in that season, we will be able to surrender that area for His deliverance and healing.

As stated earlier, at times we may feel that it would be so much easier if God would just fix everything in us in one setting and be done with it, but that would rob us of the process. The process is so important because it helps us to learn truth, humility, patience, and compassion for others. In a nutshell, the process sifts out the bad so that what is of God can be perfected.

In the process of God restoring my soul, He has also allowed me to experience compassion for the broken. For not only did I experience much brokenness and fatherlessness in the natural, but I also have four children whose father has left them in a state of brokenness. It is with this compassion that I write, knowing that God will begin to give you answers, deliver you, and bring you to an awareness of His nearness in the process, if you read this book prayerfully.

PRAYER

Father, I thank You that when life does not seem to make sense, I can always come to You for answers. You said that You know the thoughts that You think towards me. Thank you that they are thoughts of peace and not evil or bad. Please help me to always seek You in times of need to find answers. Expose every lie in my life and reveal to me Your truth. Father, please help me to not dwell on what was, but to seek You for what is. Help me to move forward in You.
In Jesus' name, amen

CHAPTER 2
Trapped in Abuse

I was born on the Island of Jamaica WI. Around the age of two, my mother left my sister and I with our grandparents and headed for the United States. My childhood memories are filled with sadness, abuse of all kinds, and rejection.

One of my early memories was when at the age of seven, a young man who lived with us raped me. As if that were not bad enough, he then took me to the pig pen and mercilessly beat me. While this was happening, I did not call for help. There was no one around to hear me but the pigs. I literally thought that this man was going to kill me and feed my body to the pigs. At the time of the incident, telling my grandparent was not even a thought in my mind because it was so shameful. The idea of them thinking that I was at fault restrained me from exposing what had happen that day. That incident set the stage for all the other situations that happened to me over the years.

After about thirteen years, our mother took us to the States. One of my first jobs at the age of sixteen was with one of the biggest food chain restaurants in America, and possibly the world, where I was gang raped by two of their employees. When the incident came to light, I was offered two weeks pay, totalling about $250, upon my leave. One of the top law firms in the state tried to represent me, but again, because of great shame, I would not follow through.

Several years later I met one of the nicest guys and we had two wonderful sons. After a while, he carried on where the other abusers left off. One particular evening, there was much turmoil between us so I did everything that I could to stay away from him. Night came and I had nowhere to go but home. After settling in the children, their father came home and beat me to the point where I felt like I was going to meet my maker. At one point he pushed me into the closet and the blows kept coming until I could not even catch my breath. In the midst of all that was going on, the thought came to mind, "Start acting crazy," and that I did. I put on such an act that I could have won an award for best actress, and with that, the abuse turned into comfort and concerns. Twisted yes, but nonetheless, it saved my life. He ended up calling 911 for me to get some speedy help. Now who could have given me a strategy like that but God? Later in my walk as a believer, I found that there is a story like mine in the bible, where King David pretended that he was mad to turned away his enemy. (1Samuel 21:13)

The next story that I want to share is that of Easter 1994. That Easter morning, my children's father trapped me in my room. The knife that I used to protect myself from him was pulled from under my pillow and held at my throat while he had me on the floor. Several times he lift the knife to stabbed me, but every time I saw his hand coming down with the knife I screamed out, "Jesus, please help me!" In every instance, I saw God pull the knife back. Although I was not in a relationship with the Lord at the time, for I had slipped back into a life of sin, He still saw fit to save my life. To Him be all glory and honor, forever and ever!

Later on, I married my children's father and had two more children, but after nineteen years of near death experiences with him, and multiple affairs, among other things, God snatched me out and hid me. After about two years of separation, he took his life and the life of another woman leaving her six children to mourn her death. His ending was painful, unfortunate, tragic, and in addition to all this were the horrible realities that he left behind for all his children to deal with.

The level of abuse that I went through was great and there is no doubt that it could have taken me out. The scar on my wrist now serves as a reminder that God has a plan for my life and no weapon that the enemy has forged against me would or could take me out prematurely. He is faithful! I could have been dead and gone many times over, but God in His great faithfulness kept me for such a time as this. Hallelujah!

Abuse is often seen as an issue that affects only those who have not encountered Christ. But in fact, many in the body of Christ have suffered or are experiencing abuse in some form as we speak. Whether it is physical, sexual, emotional, verbal, mental or otherwise, the issue needs to be addressed. Some have down played other forms of abuse, thinking that only physical and sexual counts as real abuse. Please know, any actions that forces you against your will, beats, slaps, shoves, restrains, talks down to, insults, threatens, withholds from, among other actions, should not be taken lightly. These are abuse. If you are experiencing this issue, you must no longer cover it up and carry on as if the problem does not exist. You must seek help so that you can be in a place of safety. It is God's will that you be safe.

It is said that many abused women seek help from the church because they see the church as the safe place. However, Sunday after Sunday many abused persons have left powerful services only to go back home to unpleasant situations.

Most of the abuses that I experienced were before Christ. After Christ, I did not have to deal with the physical or the sexual (with the exception of one case). However, I dealt with the emotional, verbal, and mental. Somehow, I had the notion that as long as he does not touch me, I would be ok. This mind-set was far from the truth. Although, he was not hitting me physically, the enemy was using his words and his actions to beat me down. Thus, I would feel victorious on Sunday mornings, but during the week I slumped into deep depression.

If you have experienced or are experiencing any of these unfortunate situations, it is time for your freedom. If you expect to be delivered from this situation, I encourage you to put some action to your faith. God will meet you as you move. You must say something! Seek help! After you receive help, turn around and help someone else by sharing your story. The Word of God tells us that "they overcome by the blood of the Lamb (the shed blood of Jesus) and by the word of their testimonies" (Rev 12:11). One reason why we should share our stories is so others can be encouraged, get built up, and get inspired. My testimony is that I went through tremendous abuse, but God delivered me from it all.

If you find yourself in a place where you are being abused, I encourage you to seek help. It is not and never will be God's will that anyone beat on you or degrade you. Even if it is only words, they are still degrading and damaging. You would be surprised to know the power words can have over a person's life. Do not sit under such conditions any longer. God has only good plans for your life. Not bad, not to harm you, but to bring you to an expected end.

Pray this prayer if you are experiencing any form of abuse. If not you, then pray for someone you know who is going through abuse.

National Abuse Hotline: (888) 723-4043

PRAYER

Father God, I give myself to You with all my burden cares and abuse. You said that I should cast my cares upon You because You care for me. I am asking You to give me the courage to get up and seek help. Deliver me and bring me to a place of safety. I thank You, that You only have good plans for me and not bad. You have ordained peace for me and not abuse.
Your banner over me is love. I surrender it all to You and ask You to perfect everything that concerns me. In Jesus' name I pray this, amen.

CHAPTER 3
Unmasking the Pain

O ne morning as I was in prayer, I had a quick vision where I saw a beautiful young woman. My attention was drawn to her makeup, as it was the most perfect makeup I have ever seen. Her lashes were well done with the perfect extension. However, as I glanced at her lashes, I noticed her eyes were filled with pain and tears. At that moment, I started praying for this young woman. I began to say to the Lord, "Lord, I do not know who this woman is, but you know." As soon as I said those words, I heard in my spirit, "She represents the church." I went on praying for the church/body of Christ because we are in pain, but we are great at covering up what we are going through.

One commonality I have seen among women is the ability that we have to mask our pain. The world around us could be crumbling, yet we know how to cover it up and carry on as though nothing is wrong. We have mastered the ability to cover up pain, not just physical pain, but emotional pain as well. We seem to hold the title, "The True Cover Girls." Some of us have this notion that if we show our pain we are spiritually weak. As a result we have learned how to mask the things we encounter and we have become experts in burying pain instead of dealing with them.

When my husband died, I did not go through the process of grieving. In fact, I was ashamed of anyone finding out that I really missed him. Secretly, I was hoping that God would fix him up and bring him back to me, but it went the opposite direction and this added to my pain.

For years I would look at myself in the mirror and all I could see staring back at me was pain. I thought that I was over the pain of my past, but that was not so. I would soon come to realized that the pain I carried was deeper than my experiences, it was generational. Not only did I experience pain, but so did my father, as well as his mother.

One Friday night I went to a local church and as the service progressed, it came time for personal ministry and prayer. As the call was made, I went to the alter to receive prayer. I thought that the minister would have just laid hands and prayed then move on to the next person, but it did not happen that way. The pastor laid his hand on my head and for a moment went quiet. He then said to me, "Sweetheart, you are carrying too much pain." There was no rebutal there for me, I quickly agreed and submitted myself to what the Holy Spirit wanted to do in me that night. You see, that minister had no way of knowing my history of pain, therefore, the Spirit of God had to be the one that revealed it to him, and if He revealed it to the minister, that meant that He was ready to do a work in me.

I have not been the same since then. That night the Holy Spirit started a great work in me. I can tell you now that I am not where I want to be, but I am also not where I use to be. God is still working in me today.

Perhaps you may be tempted to ask, "If God kept you through all those bad things, why did He not just prevent them from happening altogether?" That is a good question. There are times when I question the Lord about my life too. Sometimes He does not answer me right away, but as I spend time in His word, He reassures me that there is purpose in my pain.

Perhaps you are one who has experienced much pain. Do not ever feel for a moment that God has left you in your pain. Sometimes it is just a matter of you reaching out to Him. Be mindful that God is willing to help you and is waiting for you to reach out for His help. The story of Job in the *Old Testament* is a perfect example of someone who encountered a lot of pain. His wife, after seeing his pain, told him to curse God and die. (Job 2:9) For a long period of time, it would seem as if God was nowhere around to help him. Job's confession was that he looked all around and could not see nor perceived God anywhere, but he was sure that God "knew the way that [he] take." (Job 23:10) When we are dealing with issues, it may seem as if God is nowhere around, but this is not so. God is always there. God knew exactly what was going on with Job and helped him in His timing. Likewise, understand that God knows exactly what is going on with you and will help you. Your deliverance may not come when and how you think it should. For some, counseling may be the way God help you. For others He may take you through the process of deliverance. For some He may use both. Whatever the case, just know that God is perfecting and processing you, and when this process is over you will come forth as pure gold. The pain that you go through now will not be wasted. Give it to God and He will cause you to give birth to greatness for His glory.

PRAYER

Father, I am asking You to bring to the surface every deep unresolved issue that is the result of pain in my heart. I am asking you to bring inner healing in whatever form You chose. I thank You father that Jesus took stripes on His back so that I could be healed. Therefore I receive my healing by faith.
In Jesus' name, amen

CHAPTER 4
Pain With Purpose

H ave you ever taken the time to ask yourself this question, "Why did I go through the things I went through?" This question has come to my mind, especially lately. I do not believe that this question was presented to me so that I could have a pity party. Instead, it was an opportunity to investigate the true reason why the enemy tried to sabotage my future even from the womb. It has been said, "The thief does not break into an empty vault." Think about it, why were you targeted and picked on even at a young age? It is obvious that the enemy has recognized something about you that you may have not recognized about yourself. This is the reason why so many things are assigned to stop us even before we get started. If you have gone through bad situations in your lifetime, do not let the enemy use them or the memory of them to keep you down any longer. Greatness lies within you! You may not see it or feel it, but the fact that the enemy tried to destroy you simply means that there is something about you that threatens his kingdom.

There are countless examples of people in the Bible that went through severe pain and hardship and though we might question why God allowed such situations, these stories serves as examples that we have drawn strength from throughout generations.

God is usually working a far greater purpose in us than we can even fathom. The Word of God clearly states, "For our light and momentary troubles are achieving for us an eternal glory that far outweighs them all." (2 Corinthians 4:17 NIV)

To further emphasize this truth, the Word of God tells us that everything we go through will work together for our good (Romans 8:28). My understanding of this scripture is that we go through situations based on our purpose or the things for which we were predestined to do from before the foundation of the world.

While these situations are often life altering and painful, God does not leave us to work them out on our own. He is right there with us. In fact, He is never more close to us than when we call on Him in our brokenness.

> *The Lord is close to the brokenhearted and saves those*
> *who are crushed in spirit.*
> Psalms 34:18 (NIV)

God comforts us in our troubles so that when we are set free, we in turn can comfort others while they are going through their troubles.

Understand that God loves you. He did not cause anyone to hurt you the way they did. We live in a broken world with many people who are hurting. If these people do not surrender their pain to God or get professional help, they will end up hurting other people. Also, do not forget that there is a bad devil that wants to destroy God's people even before they come into the fulness of who God has created them to be. God has marked each and every one of us for His purpose and for greatness. He has an awesome plan for each one of us. Therefore, things are beginning to look up. Your troubles and your situation will not destroy you. I declare that they will make you stronger.

One passage that stands out in context to this subject is Jeremiah 29:11, "'For I know the plans I have for you' declares the Lord, 'plans to prosper you and not to harm you, plans to give you hope and a future.'"(NIV)

Know that all the negatives were not His plans for our lives, but since we have experienced them, He will develop those negative into awesome pictures of greatness and make everything work together for our good. Hallelujah!

PRAYER

*Heavenly Father, Your word declares that many are
the afflictions of the righteous, but You deliver us
from them all. Thank You for delivering me from what
could have been. Father, You know the plans that You
have for me and I thank You for they are good plans.
They are plans to bring me to a glorious future in You.
I receive your healing, restoration and deliverance
so that I can move forward.
In Jesus' name, amen.*

CHAPTER 5
A Father to the Fatherless

God intended for every one that comes to earth to come to a loving, caring family. As the result of the fall of man, God's intention for the family has been misconstrued. As a result of the lack of commitment in our family units, many of us are left with the question, "Where is my Father?"

According to *Clinton & Ohlschlager*, "Each night nearly 40% of children fall asleep in homes where their fathers are not present. The deterioration of fatherhood in America–by 72.2% of the U.S. population–is considered by some our most social ill. Encumbering the development of youth, fatherlessness promotes mental disorders, crime, suicide, poverty, teenage pregnancy, drugs and alcohol abuse, and incarceration."

It is said that a girl's father is one of the most influential people in her life, especially from birth through the teenage years. This relationship is important in that it helps us to cultivate trusting, healthy relationships. The father-daughter relationship can be the foundation for all other relationships. "When there is a healthy father-daughter relationship, it helps girls to developed into strong, confident women. A father's influence in his daughter's life shapes her self-esteem, self-image, confidence, and her opinion of men."[1]

Our parents are usually the ones who model for us what a loving, caring relation should look like. Our fathers also build the foundation for our true identity and true values, therefore, if the father is never there to begin with, how do we learn to chose with confidence or know what to look for in a spouse? According to experts, the type of men that women date and have long-term relationships with are often directly

[1] Michael W. Austin, FATHERHOOD. *Philosophy for Everyone.* <www.shrines.com/parenting>

related to the kind of relationship a girl has with her father. It is no wonder that we have so many single mothers raising children all by themselves. In many instances, it stems from the lack of a father in the mother's life as well.

Unfortunately, many of us did not grow up with our fathers. Some of us do not even have a clue what he looks like, but we have learned how to go on without him. It is no wonder we have so many young women who move from man to man. They are, no doubt, looking for someone to treat them like a good father would. Unfortunately, many times they attract young men who are also fatherless or who have no clue how to treat women.

I have observed many fatherless women who have ended up in relationships with men who do not commit the long run. This is not to say that every woman who grows up without a father cannot have a lasting relationship. They can. Instead, I am saying–if you find yourself having issues with spouses abandoning you, then go to God and let Him fill that father void and heal you.

The bible says that God is a father to the father-less. Not only that, but He promised that when our mothers and fathers forsake us, He will take us up. Therefore, when we go to God, He will lay the foundation that our earthly fathers did not lay and accurately show us who we are in Him. Furthermore, He will show us how valuable we are to Him. Ultimately, God will make us into the strong confident woman that we should be. He will also make up the difference for that which we did not receive from our earthly fathers. If you have lived your life without your natural father, know that you are not forgotten. God is about to restore your heart. He is about to reveal to you His love for you in ways that you have never imagined. He is now healing you of the father wound that you have been carrying. Be restored in Jesus' name.

PRAYER

Father God, You promised in your word that when my father and mother forsake me You will take me up. I am asking You to heal me from every form of abandonment and rejection. I pray that You will cause me to experience Your abounding love and acceptance. In Jesus' name, amen.

CHAPTER 6
Rejections

Rejection affects people in many different ways. Some of the ways that we recognize rejection in ourselves and others is when there is an inability to give or receive love. Often, when someone finds themselves being hurt or rejected repeatedly by other individuals, they put up walls. These walls are often to protect themselves from experiencing further injury to the soul. However, these walls can keep out those who are genuine and could be beneficial to the relationship. When this person finally connects, it is usually with someone who struggles with the same issues, thus making them dangerous for each other.

Rejection is feeling insecure or withdrawn. When someone is insecure they really are not sure of who they are. They tend to second guess themselves and depend on others to make decisions for them; fearing that they will make the wrong decision. In some cases, individuals overcompensate to cover up, hoping that others will not recognize their issue. In other cases, some individuals retreat or run in order to spare themselves the trouble altogether. I remember a time when I was living in Georgia, someone approached me and offer me the opportunity to connect with a group of ladies that were well established. Some were authors, others were in theatrical plays, while others were entrepreneurs. When it was time for me to exchange information with this lady, I took hers and deliberately gave her wrong information about myself. I was super conscious that these ladies would recognize my deficiencies and imperfections, so I ran. If the feeling of insecurity was not present at that time, I would have seen this as an opportunity for advancement, or at least, divine connections. The scripture that comes to mind in this case is James 1:8, it is the case of the double minded man, full of instability. More than likely, many people find themselves in this very situation. They give up great opportunities because of insecurities.

Another way to recognize rejection is being suspicious, self rejection, and being fearful of man, among many others. As stated earlier, fathers are responsible for setting proper foundations, not only in the form of provision and protection, but also in passing down real identity and true values. This could be one reason why many women are affected by rejection. Not only are some women troubled with rejection from the lack of a father, but also, some have attracted spouses who ends up abandoning them, thus leaving them to deal with multiple layers of rejection. Each time a relationship, be it intimate or otherwise, does not work out, we make the assumptions that we are unwanted or not loved. Some of us have even believed the lie that we are not good enough, therefore justifying the abandonment.

In other cases, a person may be thinking, "I was not abused or abandoned, my husband did not leave me, so why am I experiencing this rejection?" Perhaps it could be identified as *Prenatal Rejection*. This rejection comes from the womb. Any negative action that would indicate a pregnancy being a burden will send messages to that child that they are unwanted, thus rejection sets in.

If we do not receive our healing and affirmation from God, the cycle just keeps repeating itself. Rejection opens the door for other spirits to come in and destroys our lives.

One of the brutal things about this spirit of rejection is that it will cause other people, especially those who struggles with rejection themselves, to reject you. The painful part about this is that it also comes through other believers. If you do not know who you are in Christ and are not rooted and grounded in God's love, you will end up in the fight to believe that you belong to God or that He loves you.

Case in point, I was attending a bible school in Atlanta and the teacher was teaching a class on spiritual warfare. I noticed that throughout all the classes she kept looking at me. Although I was sitting on the edge of my chair taking in all the information that she was sharing, I could not help but noticed the discomfort I felt at her constant stare. At the end of one of the classes, the teacher told a story to the class about a young lady that attacked her in one of her services. Her constant stare at me became so obvious to the class as she told the story that at the end of the class, everyone moved away from me. In fact, the very friend that I went to class with that day pulled away and unfortunately, she was my ride home. I did not even get a chance to walk out the door of the classroom before I burst into deep, uncontrollable tears. In my mind, I kept on asking God , "What did she see in me that caused her to associate me with her attacker?" I could only imagined that because I sat on the edge on my seat, the fear that I was going to jump up and go at her probably played over and over again in her mind. Unfortunately, from that incident, I was scarred all over again. This time the fear of rejection from leaders attached itself to me. That spirit followed me for a long time and if it even seemed like another woman in the church was showing signs of rejection towards me, I would just run. I walked around for years expecting leaders to reject me because of that one incident.

Just because someone has rejected you does not mean that something is wrong with you. Yes, it could mean that you need deliverance from the spirit of rejection yourself, but it could also mean that God does not want you to connect with this person. One way or the other, it will not hurt to expose that rejection to the Spirit of God and let Him do whatever is necessary for you to get your complete healing. As a result of what has happen to me in the past, I have exposed my issues with rejection to Him and asked Him to heal me and He has. Even when God has delivered us from rejection it will still try to show up. This is to see if it can gain entry back into our souls. I find that when rejection rears it's ugly head, all we have to do is to spend time in God's presence. He strengthens our souls and lifts our heads. I encourage you, once you have received your deliverance, keep that space filled with the word of God so that rejection does not have any form of access to your soul.

We must be very careful that we are not rejecting or damaging the people that God loves. If we find ourselves doing so, it simply means that we need to surrender that part of us to God again so that He can complete the healing process. The Word of God tells us that love covers (1 Peter 4:8; Proverbs 10:12). When we love those whom God loves, it will be easier for us to see Christ in them, instead of demons.

At the same time, we must use wisdom in not laying ourselves careless for the enemy to attack. More importantly, we must learn to realize that we do not wrestle with flesh and blood, therefore, we respond wisely when it comes to God's people.

God has given some of us the gift of discerning of spirits, but it is not just for us to see demons in people and shun them, no! It is so that we can pray for people and help them get free.

God loves people and unfortunately, many of His people are bound up with all kinds of demonic spirits. When we as believers spend time with God and not just operate from our gift, then we will begin to have compassion on God's people and will want to see them delivered.

It is important to remember, when you and I see someone in bondage to all kinds of demonic spirits, they are being tortured and tormented by these things. For this reason, we as children of God should not add to their misery by rejecting them. Instead we should be moved with compassion and pray for them. We are ambassadors of the Kingdom and we are to bring the Kingdom of God to people where they are. When we begin to walk in love, towards all men, we will pray for one another at the drop of a hat. Much like the body, if a foot or even a finger hurts, it affects the entire body, and so it is with us in the body of Christ; if one member is hurting then it affects the entire body.

MY PRAYER FOR YOU

If you are struggling with rejection today, I pray that the love of God envelops you, that He will reveal to you the depth of His love for you. Moreover, I pray that you will know that you are accepted in the beloved. You are not unwanted. God has placed you on this earth for His divine purpose. He loves you with an everlasting love and nothing and no one can changed that.

I pray the peace of God in your spirit, in your mind and on your body. I declare that you will not stay in darkness, but that you will experience the true love and light of Jesus Christ in your heart.

In the name of Jesus, I command this power of rejection to be broken off from your life in the Mighty name of Jesus the Christ. Amen!

YOU PRAY

Father, I ask You to help me to forgive everyone who has rejected me in the past. Help me to develop a prayer life that will allow me to pray for them continually, until I have released them totally. Lord, it is obvious that they have no clue how much they are hurting others. I pray that You would heal each of them from rejection, that they too may have an encounter with You. Let them experience Your unending love and acceptance.
In Jesus' name, amen!

CHAPTER 7
True Affirmation

We all have the need to know that we are valuable, loved, and that we belong. When we are not affirmed in this way, we tend to feel isolated, estranged and rejected.

The people around us can dramatically impact our lives depending on whether or not they affirm us. God puts people in families or generations in order for them to have a sense of belonging.

This could be one of the reasons why there is such an attack on the family. If the father is taken out of the picture, they will not be able to lay the proper foundation with their children, thus we have a whole generation with no sense of belonging. So we have multitudes of mothers trying to carry on the family without one of the most important people, the father.

Jesus, being the Son of God, received affirmation from His Father in Heaven. After He had been baptized by John, while He was praying, the heavens opened and the Holy Spirit came down on Him in "bodily form like a dove. And a voice came from heaven saying, 'You are my Son, whom I love; with you I am well pleased.'" (Luke 3:21 NIV)

Now, if Jesus, who was all God, received affirmation from His father, how much more should we be affirmed. We all want to know that we are valued by others. No matter how strong and bold we may feel, we still have the need to know that someone loves us and is pleased with us.

Unfortunately, many of us do not have access to an earthly father. Maybe he was never there or perhaps he has passed on. If you are in any one of these categories, know that all is not lost. We have a Heavenly Father who loves us with an everlasting love. He will never leave us, nor will He forsake us. He chose to stay with us forever, because He loves us.

RELATIONSHIP OR RELIGION

What is the basis of your relationship with God? Is it built on a solid foundation of a true relationship with Christ or is it religion? Countless numbers of us have tried getting into the right standing with God by our works. Some of us have done the religious things, thinking that it is enough to get God to love us. We have preached, run revivals, attended church on a weekly basis, taught Sunday school classes, gone on missionary trips, among other things, without a true knowledge of God's love. God's love is the foundation that we build our relationship on. The Word of God declares,

> *For God so loved the world that he gave his one*
> *and only son, that whoever believes in him*
> *shall not perish, but have eternal life.*
> John 3:16 (NIV)

Many of us know in our mind that God loves us, but if we have not experienced this truth in our hearts, it is safe to say that we have become religious and legalistic. Truth be told, one can only have a true, loving relationship with someone that they know. Knowing God takes effort on our part. Even in a natural relationship, it takes us spending time talking and learning about the other person before we can say that we have a relationship with them. So it is with God. We have to spend time talking to Him, and He to us, before we can say we have relationship with Him. The more we get to know Him, the more we love Him and understand His love for us. If we do not know that God loves us, what we claim to have will be coming out of our heads rather than our hearts.

We may have even made requests to God and have not received anything, because we have not approached Him with the confidence that He loves us and is hearing us (1 John 5:14). Not that God will not give us our desires because we do not know Him, instead, it is because He does not want us to miss out on the greatest treasure which is a true relationship with Him.

In the back of our minds, some of us believe that God is just like our natural fathers He is not there! We may have believed that He is upset with us or He really does not care about us. Even some of the prayers that we have prayed are but mere words, born out of religious tradition. Could this be one of the reasons why the Lord complains that His people worship Him with their lips, but their hearts are far from Him? (Matt. 15:8; Is. 29:13).

God will never treat us like we do not exist or we do not matter. He cares so affectionately for us, so when the natural father drops us He steps in and says, "I will be a father to you." Therefore, know that whether or not you have a father in your life, God is your Heavenly Father who loves you so much!

One of the things I shared in the first chapter was how I often addressed Jesus, Savior, Lord, and had no problem addressing God; however it was never comfortable for me to address God as Father. I may have used "father" at the beginning of my prayers, but that was learned habit. It did not have much significance to me.

In the process of communicating my concerns to God, it reverberated back in my ear while saying God, Lord, and Jesus. It was as if the Lord was pointing out to me that I did not recognize Him as my father. One morning while I was in prayer, the Lord reminded me of a dream that He had given me. In this dream I was in a tall house. My apostle walked into the dining room and as he walked up to greet me, I responded in an awkward way. Understanding that I did not know how to respond to a father's embrace, he bypassed all that, pulled me close to him and laid my head on his chest. When he did that, I felt things break and fall off of me. In the dream, I fell to the floor under the power of God and wept uncontrollably as I felt a sense of freedom and release.

As the Lord dealt with me in prayer several days later, He reminded me of the dream. He showed me that I still had issues that limited my ability to receive His love. This dream was really not about my apostle and me. Instead, it was about God working in me to receive His loving embrace and deliverance from my past issues.

PRAYER

Father, help me to realize that I am valued and loved by You. Where I have had issues of not knowing that I am loved in the past, help me to come to the knowledge of that truth. Lord, please help me to build my relationship with You based on the truth that I am loved, accepted and valued by You. Help me to walk in confidence, knowing that I'm a daughter of the King. In Jesus' name, amen!

CHAPTER 8
Abba Father

Every now and then, we see programs on TV that show some of the most unfortunate situations with children all over the world. Many times these children are abandoned, sometimes lost, and most times they are hungry and are suffering malnutrition, even to the point of death. The grim reality is this if no one steps in to help these children, then they suffer and eventually they die.

In like manner, we were lost and dead in our sin and trespasses, but God considered us, even in our worst condition. He did not just leave us where we were, but He indeed rescued us. Not only have we been rescued, but we have also been adopted or grafted into the family of God. Now that we have been grafted in, it is important that we know who we are and whose we are.

The word adoption comes from the old French word *adoptare*, meaning, "to chose for one's self." This is what the Word of God says; "He predestined us for adoption as sons through Jesus Christ, according to the purpose of His will" (Ephesians 1:5 ESV). With this truth, we must come to the understanding that God loves us and has grafted us into His family, because He really wanted to.

God chose us in Him from before the foundation of the world. Begin to let your heart steep in this truth, that you were with Him before He formed you in your mother's womb. He says that He foreknew you, and if He did, then you must have been with Him in spirit form before you came to the earth. See, we are spirits. We only enter the body when we were conceived in our mother's womb. The fact that you and I are here in the earth simply means that God chose us and sent us to this earth for such a time as this. Never see yourself as a mistake or a misfit. You and I are here on purpose, God's purpose. We are wanted, we are valued, we have true purpose in Christ.

Now, we must make it a habit to counteract the lies of the enemy with the truth of God's word. From here on, we must begin to use the truth that we know and understand to build up ourselves, much like that house that is built on the solid rock. (See Matthew 7:24-27) I say this because the enemy will set up situations in order to trip us up and make a lie look real. Sometimes he will have the very people who seem to have a relationship with God reject us. When that happens, it will seem as if that is how God feels about us also.

In fact, sometimes we find ourselves struggling with people and situations without knowing the depth of why we struggle. Sometimes it is not people that we are worried about not liking us, because God knows, some people will not like us no matter what. Most often we are more disturbed deep in our hearts when we believe that God does not like us. Yes, in general, He loves everybody including you and I, but does He really like me? You see, what we are worried about is if God does not like me, then He will not be quick to help me. He will be quicker to make others prosper, but me? I will have to fast forty days, and make sure that I never miss church, not even one Sunday. This is the spirit of condemnation in full force. This forces us to be religious. We find ourselves doing things in order for God to like or love us. The sad truth is, this disturbing lie has affected so many of us. To make matters worse, we have mastered the art of pretending and this is why we have not been seeing the level of freedom that we ought to be seeing in the body of Christ. We love to wear masks. The Word of God says we are not condemned because we are in Christ. Therefore, when condemnation comes, whether by other believers, the enemy's voice or even the voice of our flesh, we have the power to shut it down. (See Romans 8:1)

The enemy has a way of capitalizing on our ignorance. If we do not realize that once we are in Christ, we are exempt from condemnation, the enemy will continue to use it against us. Therefore, if we do not come to the realization that we have a real Father in Heaven who loves us and has grafted us into His family and has not condemned us, then we will miss out on God's best for our lives.

God has given us all the truth that we need to live this life. We cannot continue to live in a state of ignorance for it is truely not bliss. In fact, we are destroyed for the lack of knowledge according to Hosea 4:6. How do we know that God loves us and has given us authority over condemnation? This is what the Word of God says,

> *If anyone acknowledges that Jesus is the Son of God,*
> *God lives in them and they in God. And so we know and*
> *rely on the love God has for us.*
>
> 1 John 4:15-16 (NIV)

The bible says that God lives in us and we in Him. Why would He live in someone that He does not like? Make continual declarations to yourself. Tell yourself, "God loves me and He likes me too. He is in a good mood when it comes to me because I am pleasing to my Father. Amen!"

THE VISION

One evening as I was in prayer, God gave me a vision. I was looking at a little girl playing in her father's lap. I did not see the father's face. All I saw was the beautiful little girl just playing and the father sat there enjoying their time together. As I came out of the vision I asked the Lord, "What was that about?" Strange enough, the first thought that came to mind was the voice of condemnation telling me that God was trying to tell me that I am not praying, instead, I was playing. Then the thought came to mind that maybe I should be praying for that little girl, maybe she was in danger. I chose to not go with those voices. Instead I asked the Lord to make plain to me what He was saying. The Lord made me understand that the little girl was me and He was the father. He was showing me the depth of His love for me and that I actually had an audience with Him. That vision gave me confidence in the Father's love for me. It also showed me that my Father likes me too.

More often than not, we have settled for defeat and have lived as victims, not trusting God. Most times, it is the result of not understanding that God is our abba and that he loves us no matter what.

God is a responsible father. He protects and provides whatever it is that we need. He will never be unable to provide for or protect His own. Our negative belief system has kept us in bondage, but faith in the love of God will cause us to walk in a new level of freedom.

For the sake of illustration we will look at two different stories to show a picture of Abba and His love for His beloved ones. These stories will show us that whether or not we can see God's hand at work in our lives, He loves us and is with us.

The first story is that of David. He obviously had situations and enemies that were too strong for him. With confidence he called for his Heavenly Father (Abba) to rise up and fight his enemies. David did not sit and have a pity party or complain that God must have been punishing him for something he had done wrong. The amazing thing in this situation was that the Lord did exactly as David asked Him to do. He tore the heavens and came down to defend His beloved. (See Psalms 17) David apparently knew the power of sonship. He knew that no earthly father in his right mind would watch on and do nothing as his son or daughter's life was being destroyed by their enemies. How much more will our Heavenly Father do whatever is necessary to protect us, His beloved daughters?

The second story is that of Jesus in the Garden of Gethsemane. He was sorrowful to the point of death about going to the cross. He told His disciples to stay at a certain place and watch, while He went on a little further to pray. Jesus prayed, "Abba, Father, everything is possible for you. Take this cup from me. Yet not what I will, but what you will." Mark 16:36 (NIV)

This situation was obviously overwhelming for Jesus, but when He cried out to Abba, He got a different response than David did. Certainly, God did not love David more than He did Jesus. Instead, the answer was in the purpose for His situation.

It is safe to say that no situation can hold a child of God in bondage if we learn to cry out to Him. This is what the Word of God says,

The Spirit you received does not make you slaves,
so that you live in fear again; rather the
Spirit you received brought about your adoption
to sonship. And by him we cry, 'Abba Father'
Romans 8:15 (NIV)

WE HAVE AN AUDIENCE WITH HIM

God has put His spirit (the spirit of sonship) in us and that spirit gives us access to Him. Anytime we call on our Father, access to His help is automatically granted. Now, just as in the two different cases, if what is affecting us is not God's will, He will rescue us when we call on Him, but if the situation will ultimately work out for our good and God's glory, then He will give us the grace to endure it. The point that I want to make is this—you can always call on Abba, no matter what the situation is, because you have an audience with Him.

PRAYER

Abba Father, I thank You that You have rescued me
from death and bring me into life eternal. I thank You
for adapting me into Your family, not because You had
to, but because You really wanted to. Not only do You
love me Abba, but You like me too. I am thankful that
I am pleasing to You. Help me to always trust in Your
love for me and to always rest in You, knowing
that you have my best interest at heart.
In Jesus' name, Amen!

CHAPTER 9
Comfort My People

Does God want His people to live in a state of continual discomfort? The answer is no! This is the reason He has ordained peace for us as believers. Unfortunately, so many of us have found ourselves at this place of continual discomfort, without knowing how to get relief.

Dictionary.com defines *comfort* as "to console or soothes; to bring cheer to." It is also a state of physical or psychological ease often characterized as a lack of hardship.

We all seek to be comforted, but it is not very often that we seek it from the right source. Many seek comfort in food, sex, drugs, alcohol, and all manner of other things. The truth is, any comfort we seek apart from healthy, Godly comfort will not bring satisfaction. This only gives a temporary fix to a lingering problem. This is the reason why many have to go back over and over again to be fixed. We have people who are addicted to bad habits, not because they are bad people, but much more that they seek comfort from the wrong source and became addicted. You will find that many people end up in rehab, weight loss clinics, hospitals, and sometimes unfortunately death, all in the name of comfort. Right now, as we speak, the hospitals, clubs, bars, and prisons are filled with people whose intention is to seek comfort, but instead they found nothing but more sorrow, pain, bondage and death.

Speaking of discomfort, many of us are crushed and bruised because we were not handled with care. Someone had no idea of how valuable we were. They did not realized that we were God's treasures, God's masterpieces, fearfully and wonderfully made, so they rejected us, beat us, cheated on us, used words to degraded us, kick us to the curb, and abandoned us, but God is saying, "Comfort! Comfort my people!" You see, God is the God of all comfort. No matter what the discomfort, disease, or distress is, God has the remedy for it. He is the only one who can bring true, permanent answers to your problems.

SPEAK COMFORT TO MY PEOPLE

'Comfort, yes, comfort my people!' says your God.
'Speak comfortably to Jerusalem, and cry out to her,
That her warfare is ended'
Isaiah 40:1-2 (NKJV)

Now this is the Word of the Lord that was given to Jerusalem while they were in exile. The Lord was about to end their period of exile and restore comfort unto them. In the same manner, God is about to deliver you and restore you to a place a comfort. Your deliverance comes as the Word of the Lord is released into your broken heart. Your soul is being restored as the Lord releases His spirit to heal you. I speak healing and restoration to your body and soul, in Jesus' name, amen!

YOUR WARFARE IS OVER!

You may have gone through a long period of hardship and probably are wondering if God even remembers you. The people around you may have judged you based on your hardships and concluded that your life has amounted to nothing. They see you at the bottom of life and do not see you coming up anytime soon. The enemy may have being taunting you and telling you that there is no help for you in God, but know that the Devil is a liar! God will deliver! He is the one who lifts your head. I declare to you that your warfare is over! It has ended! You are in a season of restoration. God will amend for lost time, lost relationships, lost money, lost reputation, lost health, and lost hope. He is repairing, restoring, and renewing everything in you and around you. The Spirit of the Lord is doing this! Everything that is standing in your way, God is moving by His spirit. The desert situation, God is pouring water on your dry ground. He is taking you out of the wilderness. The wilderness was for a purpose, to teach you and prepare you to stand in your place of greatness.

Therefore, do not despise your wilderness seasons. Jesus, before He started His public ministry, had to do the wilderness session. This was God's order. This time was not meant to destroy Him, instead to fortify Him and to strengthen His walls. Yes, He was God, but He was also one hundred percent man. Think about it. Although the wilderness period may be hard, our hope comes from the fact that Jesus was our greatest example on how to survive the wilderness. God is always with us in the wilderness. Know that God is here to do great things in your life. You make the path straight. Open up and allow Him to do what He does best.

PRAYER

Father, please forgive me for the times that I have sought comfort in things and from people. I realize that true comfort comes only from Your Spirit.
I ask You to fill me and heal every wounded and discomforted area in my life. Cause me to walk in total wholeness, and true fulfillment.
In Jesus' name, amen!

CHAPTER 10
The Time to Heal

I remember my very first day of training in the hospital. The doctor asked me to assist him while he attended to his patient's wound. Now if you are a nurse, or maybe one who has worked in a hospital setting, then you may know what a wound or a decubitus ulcer looks like. This was my very first time on a hospital floor as a nursing assistant and as we entered the patient's room, I was taken back by the sight and smell of rotten flesh. In fact, because of this experience I could not eat meat for about a month, that is how gross the wound was to me. I remembered the crying and groaning that came from the patient as the doctor cleaned her wound until all you saw was healthy, bleeding flesh.

Now, the doctor did not leave the wound as is, hoping that it would heal with time, nor did he clean the wound to cause further pain. Instead, this was done to cause a healthy progression of healing to the affected area.

When we talk about healing, we are not just talking about the physical, we are also talking about the emotional. Studies have shown that emotional wounds often are associated with physical ailments. For example, diabetes is rooted in rejection, self-hatred or guilt. Cancer is rooted in bitterness, unwillingness to forgive and slander of the tongue. These are just a few.[2]

In some cases, the physical illnesses may be the result of eating the wrong foods, which is still sometimes the case of emotional disturbances. One way or another, we must seek to be free and be healed from all these wounds, both physical and emotional.

There is a popular saying that time heals all wounds, but I am not so sure that this saying is true. There are multitudes of us who have been

[2] John Eckhardt, *Prayers That Rout Demons* pgs. 90,91

wounded from childhood. We thought that we would have been healed by now, but instead of healing we have become a wound magnet. Time did not do the job. It only allowed us to mask and bury our pain deeper and deeper.

Truth be known, healing is always available to the children of God, for by the stripes of Jesus we were healed. (1Peter 2:24) The sad reality is this—we do not always receive what has been made available to us because of ignorance or laziness.

God has appointed a special time to bring healing to the areas of brokenness in our lives. Our souls are not graveyards for pain; therefore, we must no longer bury the pain we feel. Instead, we must now allow God to start healing us. We are not what we went through. We are daughters of the King. I encourage you to yield everything that you have gone through to Him, the hurts, disappointments, rejection, lacking or whatever your situation may be, for NOW is your time for healing.

As you are reading these words, know that God has appointed this time for you. Although you may still be dealing with some issues, it does not mean that healing is not taking place. Healing can start off being very painful and it may even seem as if it is getting worse instead of better, but we do not walk by what we see, we walk by faith.

Dealing with past issues is often hard. We tend to feel that they are too painful to rehash, so we keep them buried.

Before any healing can take place, we must first allow God to bring to the surface the things that we are reluctant to deal with. At the moment of confrontation, the pain may feel just as fresh as when you first encountered the problem, but know that they are only coming up so that they can be dealt with. It amazes me how the Lord still bring things to the surface that took place from the time I was seven and eight years old, and when He does the Holy Spirit also walks me through the process of forgiving, letting go, renouncing, and receiving my healing.

Ask God to show you what painful emotions you are masking. When He brings them to the surface, allow Him to get them out and walk you through your healing.

This is what Jeremiah 33:6b (NIV) declares, "I will heal my people and will let them enjoy abundant peace and security."

PRAYER

Father, You have said in Your word that healing is the childrens bread. I am Your child, therefore, I ask You to bring healing to every area of my life; even the parts that I have buried. I give to You every childhood pain, every form of bad treatment, and every disappointment. I give You the permission to do whatever it takes to bring me to the place of wholeness. In Jesus' name I pray, amen.

LET IT GO

There are detriments in holding on to something when we should be letting go. If we are holding on to these old memories, old pains, and people who have hurt us, our hands are not free to receive what is new. The time is now for the Daughters of Zion to let go of all that keeps us in bondage to our broken past. Arise, shake off the dust, drop the baggage, put the weights down, stop the sins. Let it go! Stop rehearsing what he did to you, what they said, who accused you. Forget about who looked at you badly. Never mind who said you were not good enough, not qualified enough, or does not fit the profile. Forget about who left you or who was never there to begin with. It is all a trick to keep you from moving foward. The Word of God says, " Therefore, since we are surrounded by such a great cloud of witnesses, let us throw off everything that hinders and the sin that so easily entangles, and let us run with perseverance the race marked out for us." (Hebrew 12:1 NIV). This life is a race. Sometimes it is a walk, but whether we are running or walking, it will be uncomfortable with baggages and extra weight.

Sisters, the Lord is saying, let it go! Move forward! Behold I am doing a new thing, and now it shall spring forth. We must understand that it is hard to experience the new if we hold to the old. We surely do not want to miss what God is doing in this season, for it is great. The true sons of God are about to be manifested with power and strength to accomplish great and marvelous things and we are a part of that. Now, when I say sons of God, this is not gender specific. It simply means God's children walking in the spirit of God and manifesting the kingdom. God wants to heal you, restore you, strengthen you, and pour His anointing in you so that He can use you as His anointed vessel. God loves you and He is for you. Let It Go! Move forward!

PRAYER

Father, there are some things that I am holding on to that are preventing me from moving forward in You. I surrender every area of hurt and disappointment to You and I am asking You to help me to forgive. When my heart is overwhelmed, please lead me to the Rock, which is Jesus Christ. Lord, I realize that if I do not forgive and let the bad memories go, I am only holding myself back. So please work in me so that I can forgive and let it go. In Jesus' name, amen.

CHAPTER 11
You Are Surrounded

Most mornings after dropping my children off at school, I would sit in my car and have conversations with the Lord. One morning, I sat and wondered, "Where is Jesus in my life?" What I really meant was, "How do I view Him as it relates to our relationship?"

That morning I picked up my Bible and read John chapter 6. As Jesus talked about Him being the bread of life, my heart was stirred to make sure that Jesus had His rightful place in my life as Lord. Although I had conversations with Him that morning, I could not help but notice that the Holy Spirit's presence was not felt any where around.

I left the car and came into the house where I struggled in my decision to pray. That morning as I position myself for prayer, I made this statement, "Father, I really do not sense your presence right now." Right then the Holy Spirit reminded me that we do not walk by what we see or feel, but by faith. His spirit is always present, because He promised in His word that He would never leave us nor forsake us. Thanks be to God that the Holy Ghost led me into prayer that morning because when I heard those word, I recognized that the Holy Spirit was saying that we should not wait until we feel something before we pray. Our prayers should be a devotion to the Lord whether or not we feel Him. Moreover, they should be an act of faith.

In that moment the Holy Spirit reminded me of something He said to me via devotional the day before. He said, "I am beside you! Practice calling my name, (Jesus) not that you will summon me when you call my name. Instead, it will help you to realize that I am with you."[2]

[2] A.J. Russell, GOD CALLING.

In a previous chapter, I mentioned how I viewed God and His activities in my life, but this time I needed to locate Jesus and the Holy Spirit and their activities in my life also.

As I sought to locate Jesus, the lights came on. I was seated in Him! (Ephesians 2:6) He then reminded me that His spirit was in me. (Christ in me, the hope of glory. Col. 1:27) Furthermore, the Holy Spirit is the one who leads us and guides us into all truth (John 16:13). If the Holy Spirit is leading and guiding, then He is before us to lead and behind us to guide at the same time.

Wow! As the Spirit of God began to put the puzzle together for me, the revelation that I was surrounded by the Father, the Son, and the Holy Spirit burst open in my spirit. The Spirit of the Lord reminded me that very morning while I was coming back from my daughter's school that He had promised me that He would be with me wherever I go.

As I thanked the Lord for making this truth real to me, He took me back to 2010 when I was asked to work a case caring for a handicapped client. This particular assignment aggravated me at first because it was a far distance, paid very little, and it was only for one day. I did take the assignment and it was a hard case, nevertheless, I did my best at taking care of the client. Almost at the end of my assignment, while I was putting my patient back in the bed, he started prophesying to me. (Yes, the handicapped patient who never said a word to me the whole time that I was there, except for that moment.) These are the words that he released from his mouth to me, "So do not fear, for I am with you; do not be dismayed, for I am your God. I will strengthen you and help you; I will uphold you with my righteous right hand." (Isaiah 41:10 NIV) When I heard those words coming from his mouth, I actually froze. It was amazing! There was no doubt that it was the Spirit of God talking to me. My spirit was rejuvenated, ignited, and I was thankful that I went.

If the question was asked of you, "Where is Jesus in you life?", could you locate Him? The truth is this, once you have acknowledged that Jesus is the Son of God and believe that God sent Him as an atoning sacrifice for your sins, then you are saved (1John 4:10, 15). But to make it more clear, the Word of God says:

That if you confess with your mouth the Lord Jesus and believe in your heart that God has raised Him from the dead, you will be saved. For with the heart one believes unto righteousness, and with the mouth confession is made unto salvation.

Romans 10:9-10 (NKJV)

The issue with many of us is that once we have passed from death to life, we leave Jesus out of the equation. Although He has done and still is doing so much for us, we have left Him in the background.

One of the reasons why the Lord allowed me to share these stories with you is so that you could take the time to recognize yourself that God is with you. No matter what you have been through in the past or what is going on with you now, know that the Father, Son and Holy Ghost surrounds you. Although the triune God surrounds us, He still gives His Angels charge over us (Psalm 91:11). (See Matthew 28:20, Heb, 13:5, 1Cor, 3:16, Romans 8:38-39, Rev, 3:20, Eph, 3:17, Psalm34:7)

Know that even in the times when it feels like God is not with you, He is there. Sometimes He will allow His presence to not be felt so that we can seek after Him. To tell you the truth, once you have experienced God's presence, you will not want to live without continuously experiencing Him.

In the same way that He has reminded me of these truths, I am now reminding you also. Practice calling His name, not so that you can summon Him, rather, as a reminder that He is near at all times. Sometimes you may not feel His presence, but know that we do not operate by feeling. God is a spirit and although we can feel Him, He does not want us to operate out of our natural senses. We know that He is with us because He says it, and whatever God says, it is so. No matter what!

PRAYER

Father God, I thank You that no matter what I am going through right now, I am surrounded. You go before me to make crooked places straight and You are my rare guard. I am seated in Christ and am hidden in your secret place. Where can I go from your presence Lord? I thank You that wherever I go, You are there. Thank You for giving me such protection.
In Jesus' name I pray, amen!

NOTES

You have completed **PART I** of this book and read some of the situations that have caused much pain and severe brokenness in my life. Please allow God to bring to light the things that have been a source of pain to you. Take the time to pray and list the things that the Holy Spirit reveals to you, then ask God to begin healing your heart.

_____

_____

_____

_____

_____

_____

_____

_____

_____

_____

_____

_____

_____

_____

_____

_____

_____

_____

NOTES

NOTES

PART II

CHAPTER 12
You Are a Deliverer

Many of us have gone through being wounded, coupled with pain and the setbacks that it brings, but now that God has healed us, it is time to move to the next phase of our lives. God wants to move us from a place of brokenness and obscurity and transition us into the glorious future that He has ordained for us. Now is not the time to sit in the background, waiting on man to validate or approve you and I, because God has approved us.

Think about it, can you imagine the amount of time we have wasted waiting on human beings to approve us? We miss God at times, wondering what this person will think or what that person may say. We sometimes spend precious time worrying about who won't accept us, therefore we miss God on many occasions.

Sometimes God will not allow man to validate us because in such case, we will always look to man and miss God. God will sometimes allow the very people that you and I look to for validation to reject us. This is not to further damage us; instead, it is to direct us to the true validator, which is God Himself.

Sometimes we may even find ourselves wanting to be like those we look up to. Now, not to say that we cannot admire the gifts, talents, and the calling that are in someone's life, but God wants every one of us to know who we are in Him and to be at peace with that. He has placed greatness in us and if no one around us sees it or recognizes it, that does not mean that we are not called to greatness.

When we speak of deliverers, Moses served as one of the greatest deliverers in the History of God's servants. However, Moses clearly did not see himself as God saw him. God saw him as the man for the job, but Moses saw himself as inferior in comparison to the task. Moses had so many rebuttals for God including, "I can't speak and what if they do not believe that you sent me?" Oh, how so many of us can identify with Moses. For although God calls us deliverers, we cannot see past our weaknesses. The song of the enemy, "I can't, what if," plays continually until we have talked ourselves out of God's assignments for our lives.

You and I must no longer use our broken pasts to keep us from what God has called us to do. For our brokenness and pain may have been orchestrated as stumbling blocks to detour or stop us, but God allowed them because with His help, they became or will become training grounds and stepping stones to build a great deliverers in His kingdom.

Look at Jesus. His training ground was all that He suffered. Can you imagine going through even half of what Jesus went through? I certainly cannot, yet the Word of God tells that Jesus learned obedience by the things He suffered. If you should ask most of those whom God has call out to serve, they will tell you that they involuntarily enrolled in the school of suffering, and suffering 101 was mandatory. Likewise, the things that you and I have gone through or are experiencing now will be our training ground to do great exploits for the Lord.

The next thought is that God sometimes allows brokenness so that His power can be seen even through our weaknesses. When God uses us, we cannot take the credit for ourselves because we know that without Him we would have remained ineffective and unable to help anyone.

Let me share a quick story with you. We were on a mission trip to Jamaica and as my sister ministered to the people in our Sunday morning service, they started getting their deliverance. Now, just to show the extent of the deliverance that was taking place, people were on the floor, slithering like snakes, and some even barked like dogs. At first glance, my thoughts were to find myself a corner somewhere and pray for the people while the Spirit of God continued do His thing. This particular Sunday morning, I stood over a lady with no confidence at all, but as I looked to God, I heard the word of the Lord come to me saying, "My Spirit is upon you to do this, for this reason you are here–to set the captives free." When I heard those words, I knelt to the floor beside another bold woman of God and we laid hands on the women and watched them get their deliverance and then fill with the Holy Spirit. After one of the services, a woman began to express to us how free she felt. She said, in fact, she had never felt such freedom before, and all this was God's power at work in spite of our weaknesses. He gets the Glory!

These are the words of Apostle Paul,

"Brothers and sisters, think of what you were when you were called; not many of you were wise by human standards; not many were influential; not many were of noble birth. But God chose the foolish things of the world to shame the wise; God chose the weak things of the world to shame the strong. God chose the lowly things of this world and the despised things—and the things that are not—to nullify the things that are, so that no one may boast before him. It is because of him that you are in Christ Jesus, who has become for us wisdom from God."

1Corinthians 1:26-30 (NIV)

Moving forward requires that you let go of your past! Let me say it another way. Stop letting your past hinder your future. I can attest to that. I was a victim for far too long. Although I had some clue that God had placed greatness in me, I had no drive or hope that anything good would happen for me. When we continue to hold on to what is behind us, it really keeps us from moving forward. This is what Paul says,

No, dear brothers and sisters, I have not achieved it, but I focus on this one thing: Forgetting the past and looking forward to what lies ahead, I press on to reach the end of the race and receive the heavenly prize for which God, through Christ Jesus, is calling us.

Philippians 3:13-14 (NLT)

When we yield all our brokenness, regrets, and our painful past to God, He heals us and uses us as His deliverers on the earth. One of the things I have not shared about that particular Sunday morning service was that there was one other minister who had recently lost her husband due to an illness. She stood up that morning and ministered on healing. In fact, the subject of healing was given to her to minister months before her husband went home to be with the Lord. After that, it would have been ok if she did not minister at all and even if she did, it was okay with us if she changed the subject altogether, but she never did. She would not allow what happened in her past to hindered what God wanted to do through her.

Also that Sunday right before all the ministering took place, a call was made for those who have experienced or are experiencing emotional issues. Shame was especially high that moment, for no one wanted to expose their issues. No one wanted to come to the alter fearing that other people in the community would know what they were going through. The Holy Spirit prompted me to share some of my stories of past abuses and to our surprise, the people began to come to the alter. Even men began to come up for prayer. In fact, the very first person that came up was a man. After that, I would say the ministering went on for at least another hour. When everything was finished, many had given their lives to the Lord, some re-dedicated their lives and many got a mighty deliverance. Do not underestimate what God will use you or your story to do.

As in the case of Moses, as he stepped out into God's assignment for his life, God backed him with some of the greatest signs and wonders that have impacted generations, including those to come. Likewise, you also step out into what God has called you to so that you can make a mark on your generation.

PRAYER

Father, I thank You that regardless of my past You have still chosen me. Please give me the courage and the strength to stand in the place where You have called me to stand. I declare Your word over my life that Your spirit is upon me to accomplish greatness.

I pray that wherever I go and whatever I do for Your kingdom, You will always be with me. I yield myself to You Lord. Use me as you please and cause me to bring Glory to Your name always.

In Jesus' name I pray, amen.

CHAPTER 13
Ministry of Compassion

The ministry of compassion is so necessary for us to truly reach people today. You can see and even feel the difference in a ministry, especially when it is coming from a heart of compassion. Have you ever had someone minister to you who had no idea what you are dealing with? They have absolutely no compassion! Their ministry would feel more like the doctor cleaning a wound to the point where it bleeds, but puts no ointment to help it heal. In like manner, so it is when we minister to the broken without compassion.

WHAT IS COMPASSION?

Merriam-Webster defines *compassion* as "a consciousness of others distress together with a desire to alleviate it."

Another source, Wikipedia, The Free Encyclopedia, defines it as, "the emotion that one feels in response to the suffering of others that motivates a desire to help." In a way, I believe that compassion and the ministry of comfort works together. One way in which to recognize compassion for others in your life is when you see someone in a situation and are moved to do something to make that person's life better or to bring them to a place of ease.

This is what our past experiences do. They help us to recognize, identify and be conscious of the situations others are going through, especially when we have gone through those same situations. Compassion is what we are feeling when we have the desire to alleviate the discomfort and distress that the person may be experiencing.

The Word of God tells us that when Jesus saw a crowd, He was often moved with compassion to feed, help, heal, or to free someone. (See Mark 1:40-41; 6:34; 8:2; 9:22 Matthew 9:36; 14:14.) Likewise, we must ask the

Lord to fill us with compassion for those whom He has allowed in our path for us to help.

I remember my first encounter with someone who had no compassion for what I was going through. I was experiencing much mental and emotional abuse in my marriage. At this particular time, the awareness hit me that no human being, especially a child of God, should be dealing with such abuse or disrespect. As a result, I called to get help in the form of counseling and emotional support. The counselor that answered the phone began to asked me some questions, but as I answered her, she became very mean. She began to ask me, "How can you sit in something like that, you don't care about yourself? Don't you have any self respect?" By the end of the call, I did not want her help anymore. She turned me off so much that I did not seek help from another counselor. The counselor more than likely meant well by what she was saying to me, but the way it was conveyed tells me that she had no compassion for people in the position that I was in. Although the things she said were all true, they did not help me, instead they caused me to retreat.

While we are on this subject of compassion, one experience comes to mind. We were on our way to prayer one Saturday morning when we saw a young lady walking. She was well dressed but there was a sense of confusion with her. We stopped and invited her to the prayer meeting, hoping that even if she did not show at prayer that day, she would at least show up on a Sunday morning.

To our surprise, she came right into the prayer meeting that morning. As we prayed, the Lord instructed the leader that we should hold hands and pray for one another. No sooner than we held each others hands did an overwhelming feeling of sorrow, rejection, pain, and worthlessness come over me. It was so intense that it felt like something pull the strength from every muscle and all that I could have done was to slump over and wept uncontrollably. Everyone that was there felt this to some extent, but for some strange reason, it hit me quick and hard. Now, at the time I had no idea why I was affected that way. I did not understand until my mother explained to me what it was.

See, for the most part of my life, before Christ and for some time after, I experienced all of those unhealthy emotions, so when this young lady came in experiencing the same emotions, I discerned them. Not only were they discerned, but my whole being responded to what she was dealing with. True intercession gushed out of my spirit for this young lady, because God had her freedom in mind. In fact, the entire group interceded for the young lady until her breakthrough came. That Saturday morning when the young lady left the prayer meeting, she looked like a totally different person. To God be all glory, for all the great things He has done!

As believers, we may all have different gifts and ministries, but we minister from the same spirit. This is why you and I should never seek to do something just because someone else looks good doing it. God has prepared a work for each of us from before the foundation of the world that we should walk in them (Eph 2:10). We are anointed for what we were design for; therefore, we have compassion for those whom we were called to. If you are called to be a teacher, do not seek to become a nurse for the fact that nurses makes more money. You will not have compassion for your patients. Your motive will not be the well being of those you are caring for, instead it will be to make more money.

Say yes to God's will for your life and let Him use you to bring compassion to those whom He has called you to.

PRAYER

Heavenly Father, I thank You for Your son Jesus Christ who showed to us the greatest example of compassion. I am asking You to give me a heart of compassion for people; especially for those whom You have called me to. Please help me so that whatever I do in this life, I show mercy and compassion to others. Fill me up with Your love in such a way that it affects the people around me. In Jesus' name I ask, amen.

CHAPTER 14
You Are Chosen

God chose us in Him from before the foundation of the world and has sent us to this earth for His purpose. For many of us, we believe that because we have gone through bad things in life, it has negated the fact that we are chosen by God. No. You have been chosen and God's purpose for your life is still waiting for you to fulfill!

Let us imagine a computer, for example. When there is too much bad memory, it slows the computer and at times will even cause it to crash. Once the computer is repaired, it begins to function as new again. It is the same with us; too many negative experiences can keep us from functioning as we should, but as the spirit of God works on us, He frees us and make us able, so that we can fulfill His purpose in the earth.

Know that God has made all things new in your life and as long as you and I say yes to Him, heaven comes in agreement to help us accomplish all that we were chosen to do.

Now is the time to ask the Holy Spirit to do a complete scan and let Him remove all that is not good for you. Come in agreement with the spirit of God and give Him full access to everything so that He can work in you. God is your repairer, restorer, and your healer. He is making all things new in your life. He will accomplished all of this by His Spirit.

Know what the Lord has said about you. He is saying that you are His treasured possession (Exodus 19:5). He has chosen you (John 15:16)! He has predestined you (Romans 8:29-30). He has made His decision about you in advance, and He has foreordained and elected you by His divine decree (1Peter 1:20). God has prepared a work for you before the foundation of the world, that you should walk in it (Ephesians 2:10). Know that His Spirit is upon you to do wonders (Acts 1:8)!

MY SPIRIT IS UPON YOU!

"The Spirit of the LORD GOD is upon me;
because the LORD hath anointed me to preach good
tidings unto the meek; He hath sent me to bind up the
brokenhearted, to proclaim liberty to the captives, and
the opening of the prison to them that are bound;
To proclaim the acceptable year of the LORD, and the
day of vengeance of our God; to comfort all that mourn;
To appoint unto them that mourn in Zion, to give unto
them beauty for ashes, the oil of joy for mourning, the
garment of praise for the spirit of heaviness;
that thy might be called trees of righteousness, the
planting of the LORD, that he might be glorified."

Isaiah 61:1-3 (KJV)

I can remember a dream that I had a while back. In this dream, we were sitting in a classroom. It was myself and a few other people. There was an instructor behind the scenes giving instructions, but I did not see him, I only heard his voice. At one point in the session, I heard the instructor say, "I am calling you out to lead the group." Once those words were released, everyone started looking at me. In the dream, I began to hide from the instructor so that he could call on someone else, but he did not. When I realized that he was waiting on me to say yes, I began to throw myself down on the floor just to show the instructor that I was not capable of this task. When I came out of the dream, there was a clear understanding of what the Lord was saying to me.

God was calling me to step out into some things, but the feeling of inadequacy attacked me. The belief that someone stronger, more versed with the word, someone who had a great command of the english language, a person who look the part, in other words, 'the bold and the beautiful', but not me. As far as I was concerned, I needed just a little more training, a mentor, more time to formulate my sentences.

I needed to live bigger, drive better, and have it all together before I could be qualified for that task. Many of you have this same mindset when it comes to saying yes to God. You may feel as if you are not the right person for the task, but know that God does not call the qualified, instead, He qualifies those whom He has called. This does not mean that you will automatically be a pro at what you do. There will be people smarter, bolder, and more eloquent than you are, but that does not disqualify you, instead, you learn as you grow.

God is expecting those that He has chosen to now arise and begin to shine. The earth is full of darkness and people are looking for hope. For many of you who are reading this book, God's spirit is upon you to do great things. God has chosen you for the task and because He has chosen you, He has put His spirit upon you to accomplish His purpose. You see, many of God's people are out there. They may not necessarily be in our churches or come to our events, but they are bound up or in bad relationships. They may be in the prisons, both naturally and spiritually. Some are held captive by sin and shame and all they need is for someone to share the gospel of Jesus Christ with them. The reason for the Spirit of God to be upon us is so that we can bring people into the Kingdom (So that they can be called trees of righteousness and the planting of the Lord.) We need not worry about not being capable, because the gospel has enough power to do what is necessary in each person that we come in contact with. Know that God does not call everyone to a pulpit ministry. You may not even be called to the five fold ministry, but make no mistake, God has called you to do something great for such a time as this ... accept the call!

YOU WILL BE CHALLENGED

When you and I are called or chosen by God, even before we accept the call, the enemy will challenge us. Prayer and the Word then becomes our greatest weapon because it strengthens us and it fortifies us so that we can withstand adversity. Jesus was one that always prayed, therefore, when the Devil challenged His identity, He was able to overcome. One of the first things the Devil will do when we are called to step out into anything great is to challenge our identities. The enemy will use anyone or anything that he can use to keep you from accomplishing your purpose.

When one is not sure they heard God, the enemy will definitely have a field day with your questioning or second guessing yourself. Do not remain in a place of doubt to what God has said because it weakens your hand and often stops you from going forward. Spend more time in God's presence so that He can tell you who you are in Him. If you know what His plans are, it will help you to overcome the challengess when they come. Refuse to retreat. Do not retreat under any circumstances. Paul puts it this way, "Therefore, my dear brothers and sisters, stand firm. Let nothing move you. Always give yourselves fully to the work of the Lord, because you know that your labor in the Lord is not in vain." (1 Corinthians 15:58 NIV)

Even when we are being challenged, it is of utmost importance that we obey God. There are two stories in the bible that I refer to every now and then when I need to obey God in His decisions. One: "The man of God from Judah" read 1 Kings 13. This is one of the best stories that I have ever read on obedience to God. Strange enough, my mother told me this story years ago before she went home to glory and it stayed with me. Even more strange, about a week before she left, we were having a conversation over the phone as we often did. In the middle of our conversation, she said to me sternly, "If God tells you to do something, and you know for sure that it is God, then do it!" In fact, she was so stern that I remained silent on the phone not saying anything for a while. All I thought in my mind at that time was, what has gotten into her, why is she so stern? I truly could not figure it out back then, but now I understand. God's orders are to be carried out no matter who believes you are not the one to do it. It is not your problem who knows your troubled past or even your present situations. Your job is to carry out what God has given you to. Know for sure that there are determents in disobeying God's order.

Two: the story of Nehemiah rebuilding the walls of Jerusalem. The enemy will use every form of distractions there is to try and stop you, but if you are faithful to answer the call and remain where God has placed you, you will overcome. (See Ch. 4:1-3; Ch. 6:1-5) When distractions do not work, the enemy will suggest lies. Sometimes even the key people in your life will appear to not like you. The enemy will even suggest that in the same way those people do not like you, that is the way God feels about you also. If we come into agreement with those lies, they will hinder us from stepping into the things that God has called us to walk in. It limits us from experiencing all that God wants us to and it tampers with the intimacy that we could have had with the Lord. Truth be known, if we believe that someone does not really like us, we will not be interested in spending time with them.

The enemy will use intimidation. When we are intimidated, we more than likely will not walk in the full authority that God has given us. It will cause what God has placed in you to remain dormant. With intimidation comes his family members, the fear of rejection and other fears. These will also stop us from walking in our God given potential. The best cure for these is to spend more time in God's presence and develop a love for His word and worship.

One of the reasons why I am inspired to encourage others in this area is because I experienced much internal turmoil when it was time for me to step out and do what God said to do. When the Lord spoke to me, I understood what He was saying because He made sure that He got the message to me in many different ways. Once I got the message, it was then time for me to move forward with it, but I had a hard time with intimidation and the fear of what others would say about me.

To tell you the truth, I still have to remind myself from time to time that God has chosen and authorized me. I still have to tell myself that I am His beloved and that He sees fit for me to represent Him. One of the things that the enemy has used against me was the fact that I was not the bold, have it together type. Every now and then I would ask the Lord, are you sure that you called me? I sometimes do not feel bold or strong, but the Spirit of God would remind me again of Moses, and not only him, but a few others also. He reminds me of Joshua 1:6, *"Be strong and courageous"* verse 7, *"Be very strong and courageous"* verse 9, *"Have I not commanded you? Be strong and courageous. Do not be afraid; do not be discouraged, for I the Lord your God is with you."*

Gideon was another example of one who did not feel strong or fit the profile for any task of God. In fact, when the angel of the Lord appeared to Gideon and called him mighty warrior, he rebuts. Judges 6:12-13, *"Pardon me, my Lord, but if the Lord is with us why has all these happen to us?"* verse 14, the Lord turned to him and said, *"Go in the strength you have and save Israel out of Midian's hand. Am I not sending you?"* The Lord knows what He has placed on the inside of everyone of us, therefore when He calls us out we may not feel strong. We may not feel courageous, we may not even feel called, but that does not negates what was set from before the foundation of the world.

PRAYER

Father, I declare Your word over my life that Your Spirit
is upon me to preach the good news to the poor.
You have sent me to bind up the broken-hearted,
to proclaim freedom for the captives and release from
darkness for the prisoners, to proclaim your favor,
and the day of vengeance of our God,
and to comfort all who mourn in Zion. I thank You
Father that You are the one who qualifies and
authorizes me. I thank You for your amazing
grace in my life, in Jesus' name.

CHAPTER 15
Time in His Presence

T ime spent in God's presence is priceless! Sometimes because we are inundated with so much noise, we cannot even hear God's voice or sense His presence. In those times we should chose to leave the television, the phone or the external activities for the sake of spending time with God. No time spent in God's presence is wasted time. In fact, one moment in His presence can do what a lifetime of toiling cannot achieve. The Word of God in Psalms 16:11 tells us that being in God's presence will fill us with Joy, and at His right hand we find pleasures forevermore. This means that whatever our hearts desire, we will find true fulfillment in God's glorious presence.

Speaking of His presence, I can remember a time when a minister asked me to come and share my testimony with the ladies in her congregation. I did everything possible to be prepared for that evening, except spending time in God's presence. I remembered being at the church and heard her briefly sharing a little of my story with the people, so one could only imagine the anticipation of the congregation to hear something powerful and impactful. As she shared about my story, she became teary eyed. If she had called me at that moment to share, I probably could have gotten by on the basis of emotions, but she did not called me then. After the minister shared, she had a brief meeting and then she called me up. By this time all the emotions I was feeling were totally gone and I was left with nothing but a dry story. The pastor gave me half an hour to let the Holy Spirit use me, but to my embarrassment, I spoke for about five minutes and shared a jumbled version of what could have been someone's deliverance. For the person in the audience who needed to hear my testimony that evening, it had been wasted. For me though, that was my first lesson on how to never minister without the presence or the anointing of God. I could not wait until the benediction was pronounced so I could run. In fact, I prayed that if anyone from that congregation ever saw me on the street, they would never recognize me. I left the church that night, went to a fast food restaurant, and bought four boxes of chicken with lots of honey. There I sat in the driveway, poured honey on my chicken and had a big pity party.

I share this story to show the importance of the presence of God in an individual's life, especially when one is ministering to people. Nothing we do for the Lord should be done without the anointing or the presence of God. When God's presence shows up while we minister, He is showing His approval of what you are doing for Him; therefore, we should stay at His feet until we are filled and refreshed so that others will be blessed by our ministering.

It is in His presence that we get our healing and our deliverance. As we seek to draw close to God, He comes closer to us. Even in times when we are suffering from all the negative emotions, finding ourselves in His presence strengthens and cause us to be resilient against unhealthy emotions. 2Corinthians 3:18 tells us that we are changed as we behold Him. It is true that whatever or whoever we focus on will be what we draw closer to, and whatever or whoever we draw close to, we become like them. Therefore, in spending time in His presence, we become like Him.

God's presence is everywhere at all times, but His manifested presence has to be invoked. When you and I earnestly seek after Him with all our hearts, He shows up in the most magnificent ways and does amazing things in our lives.

When anyone experiences the true presence of God, it brings their spirit-man to remembrances of what they lived in before they were formed in their mother's womb. In fact, we were all made to experience this beautiful presence and when we are not doing so, we will find ourselves turning to other things and people to make ourselves feel good. Of course, God does not want us to only experience His presence to just feel good. Every time He shows up, it is always to do something in us or for us.

There are times when the Lord will give us the feeling that He has pulled His presence from us, so that we can seek after Him. He also allows adversities to drive us into His presence at times. What was happening when David said these words? "You have said, 'Seek my face.' my heart says to you, 'Your face, Lord, do I seek.'" He was experiencing a lot of turmoil. He was afraid, he had many enemies and foes, war had risen against him, but the Lord reminded David that seeking His face would take care of all his enemies and bring him to a place of safety. (Psalms 27:8 ESV)

God is delighted when we seek Him. It gives Him pleasure to know that His beloved wants to spend time with Him and that we want to know His heart.

Many times, we see anointed men and women of God and want to be like them, but their anointing does not come as a result of what they know. Instead it is who they know. They have spent time in the presence of God. Please do not just read a book and feel that you are anointed, or listen to a sermon and think that you have now become anointed by what you heard. Instead, get in God's presence. Once you have experienced His presence, you will not want to live without it; in fact, you will not want to do anything without it.

One of my favorite books of the Bible is the book of Exodus. It is one of my favorites because it is filled with accounts of Moses encountering God's presence. For years I skipped over the book of Exodus and did not care to read it at all, but when I finally did, it became my favorite. Every time I would see Moses or the children of Israel encountering God's presence, it would stirred me to seek Him more. Let's take a look.

Moses' first encounter with God was really his trip down the Nile river. This was the first miraculous act in Moses' life. Think about it! Who in their right mind puts a baby in a basket and lets it go thinking that the child would be safe, unless God's presence was with that child?

Moses encountered God's presence as an adult when the angel of the Lord appeared to him in a blazing fire out of a bush (Exodus 3:2). *"Now, Moses did draw closer to the burning bush because he was curious, but when the Lord saw that he came closer to the burning bush, the Lord called to him from within the bushes."*

Sometimes God will call us come up higher when we are in the midst of experiencing fiery situations. When He allows this, it is because He wants to reveal Himself to us in ways we have not experienced before. However, if we do not draw closer to Him when He is drawing us, we will miss out on God's best and not only that, but we would have gone through our adversities in vain. We must always count it a privilege when we feel the drawing of the spirit of God. There is a passage of scripture that says, "Blessed is the man You choose and allow to draw near." (Psalm 65:4 MEV)

After we have encountered God's presence, we cannot help but burn with passion to seek after Him even more. Not only that, but spending time in His presence will move us from one level of our walk with Him to another.

The next part that stands out to me is when God decides to visit the children of Israel in an incredible way.

"The Lord said to Moses, 'I am going to come to you in a dense cloud, so that the people will hear me speaking with you and will always put their trust in you.' Then Moses told the LORD what the people had said. And the Lord said to Moses, 'Go to the people and consecrate them today and tomorrow. Have them wash their clothes and be ready for the third day, because on that day the LORD will come down on Mount Sinai in the sight of all the people.'" (Exodus 19:9-11 NIV)

There are so many messages in these words. Hearing God and knowing His voice is so important. We need to know His voice, especially in the season that we are in right now. We need to hear the voice of God in our every situation and that only comes by spending time with Him. One of the reasons why Jesus was able to say that His sheep knows His voice was because they spend time together. (See John chapter 10.)

CONSECRATION

Times of consecration are also important in experiencing the presence of God. When we take the time to consecrate for the sake of drawing close to God, He will meet with us.

Sin will block us from entering God's presence; therefore, if we are living in sin, we will not experience His presence in a tangible way. The writer of Psalms 24:3-4 asked the question, *"Who may ascend the mountain of the Lord? Who may stand in His holy place? The one who has clean hands and pure heart. Who does not trust in an idol or swear by a false god."* (NIV) God knew that He could not meet with the children of Israel in their unsanctified condition, but He wanted them to hear His voice for Moses' sake, so He gave Moses the instructions for the people to follow in order for them to experience His presence. What does it means to have clean hands? It means to be blameless or to be without sin. The only way this can happen is when we are hidden in Jesus Christ.

Another thing that we can see in this scripture was God giving us a hint about the future. The Lord is saying in this season now is the time for us to consecrate ourselves because on the third day He will come in the sight of all the people. We have already entered the third day on the Lord's calendar and we really do not know the day or the hour; therefore, we are to keep our garments clean. We need to seek God like never before because everything is changing. We are at the cusp of the return of Christ and now is not the time to sit in complacency. It is not the time to let our past hold us back. Now is the time to rise up and go after Him with all our hearts. There is work for us to do!

One of the next encounters that stood out to me is in Exodus 34 when God told Moses to cut for himself two tablets of stone so that He could re-write His laws for the people to follow. Moses broke the first ones in his anger when he learned that the people had turned from the true and living God to worship an idol. The Lord told Moses to be ready by the morning and come up to Mount Sinai and present himself there to the Lord, on the top of the mountain. So Moses rose early in the morning and went to the top of the mountain as God had commanded. There, the Lord descended in the cloud and stood with Moses and proclaimed the name of the Lord. When God proclaimed His goodness and His mercy to Moses, he bowed his head to the ground and worshiped God. In God's presence Moses was able to intercede on behalf of the people, for they had sinned against a holy God by offering sacrifices to an idol. God, in His mercy, renewed the covenant with His people all because Moses interceded for them in His presence.

There are a few things that I have gathered from reading this passage.

1. God will meet us when we set times to meet Him. I can remember listening to the radio one day and hearing a minister talk about how he shut down all media to spend time with the Lord. As a result of what he did, the Lord gave him breakthroughs and awesome testimonies. Upon hearing his testimonies, I decided that I wanted to do that too. The challenge was to take three days with no television, phones, FaceBook, Twitter or Instagram, and just time spent in His word, in prayer, and meditation (on His word). That week, I came to find out how much I was hooked on social media and did not realize it. My efforts lasted a day and a half, but truth was revealed to me in that process.

   God is not expecting us to shut down everything or put aside our daily obligations to seek after Him, however, He wants us to put Him at the center of our lives and that means setting special times to meet with Him. If you ask me, I think that God is literally delighted when we seek after Him and He rewards those who seek Him.

2. Another thing that God told Moses was to come up by himself. What this indicates is that God seeks for those who would be intimate with Him. His presence is with those who seeks Him in their private time. You can always tell the people who spend private time in God's presence because they have peace and rest, they do not have to strive for anything. When they speak or pray, you can tell that they have been with the Lord. They may not necessarily

be the loudest either, but their words carry much weight, all because they practice His presence in their private times.

3. We cannot experience God's presence if we are trying to do so for the wrong reasons. Only those with pure motives can enter the presence of God. God knew Moses' heart for the people. He knew that Moses was not trying to present Himself as superior; instead, he wanted to connect the people with God. Moses could be trusted to enter God's presence. God trust Moses with all that He did because He knew Moses had His heart for His people. As we read in Psalm 24:3-4 it says, *"Who may ascend the mountain of the LORD? Who may stand in his holy place?"* The question is answered, *"The one that has clean hands and a pure heart, who does not trust in an idol or swear by a false god."* (NIV) God is looking for those who will seek Him for true relationship, those with whom He can share His heart, those whose motives are pure towards Him. He seeks for such to come into His presence. God wants us as believers to practice His presence. It will take some effort on our part though because His manifested presence is not automatic.

The last time we see the presence of God in the book of Exodus is in chapter 40 after Moses has obeyed God in setting up the tabernacles in accordance to God's divine instruction. Verse 34 says, *"Then the cloud covered the tent of meeting, and the glory of the LORD filled the tabernacle."* We will encounter the presence of God when we walk in total obedience to God's assignment for our lives. The key word here is obedience. There is no way that we are going to walk in disobedience to God and experience His presence or His glory.

My encouragement to each and every person who reads this book is to follow hard after God. Seek to know Him. Seek to experience His presence. You will not regret it and your life will never be the same.

PRAYER

*Father God, I want to experience Your presence
in a way I have never experienced it before.
Please help me to push past all the everyday
distractions to find the time to come into Your
presence. Your word declares that in Your presence
there is the fullness of joy. I want to experience that joy
that can only comes from Your presence. Help me not
just to come in Your presence only for what I can get,
but to come in order to know You more. Please draw me
Father, and I will come after you.
In Jesus' name, amen.*

CHAPTER 16
Working the Word of God

CASTING DOWN IMAGINATION

Casting down imaginations, and every high thing
that exalteth itself against the knowledge of God,
and bringing into captivity every thought
to the obedience of Christ
2Corinthians 10:5 (KJV)

One morning as I was at my kitchen sink washing the dishes, the thought came to mind that so many believers walk around looking for deliverance when in actuality all they need to do is to continue casting down vain imaginations.

Think about it! How else will we learn how to cast down imaginations unless we come face to face with them? Our minds are truly the place where the enemy fights us; therefore, we must learn how to fight back by using the Word of God.

That day as I was on my way to work, the Holy Spirit gave me a better understanding of what He was saying to me. The enemy introduces a vain imagination, or a random thought. If we do not counter-attack right away with the truth, it then repeats itself over and over again in the mind until it becomes a thought process. At this point we can still reverse it by applying truth, but if we do nothing it then becomes a stronghold.

This means that this thing went from one random thought to a continuous thought process, then a stronghold. What the Holy Spirit taught me is this–as soon as the imagination comes, cast it down. The tricky thing about this is that one may not always recognize that the imagination is not their own thought. They will often be so subtle that you will allow it to rehearse itself in the mind.

How do I recognize a vain imagination? It is a lie! It always goes against the truth.

How do I cast it down? By using the Word of God. For example, the enemy may say something like, "God will never come through for you," or "Your situation will never change." Your response should always be, "My God shall supply all my needs according to His riches in Glory by Christ Jesus." Or we can say, "God is perfecting everything that concerns me." In the case that you did not cast it down right away, you are still able to use the Word of God to capture and reverse that thought. If we do not put a stop to the lies and leave the enemy to play with our minds, he will use what we did not capture to capture us and use those very thoughts to build strongholds in our minds.

TRANSFORMATION THROUGH THE WORD

Every chance we get, we should use the Word of God to change our negative situations. Know that the Word of God works! We can confess it, we can declare it.

Decree it, and meditate on it, among other things. The Word of God will bring tremendous transformation in our lives. It is actually impossible for us to use the Word of God on a consistent basis and not see the results in the form of change. The Word of God is so powerful that when it is mixed with faith it can change even the physical conditions.

DELIVERANCE THROUGH THE WORD

The Word of God brings deliverance. Often when it comes to our deliverance, we expect God to do it in an instant and take care of everything at one time. Yes, God can deliver us with one word or in one instant; however, it does not always happen like that. The truth is, it is as we spend time in the Word of God that our freedom comes.

When I think about the Word of God setting people free, I think of a container filled with dirty water. If you should begin to pour clean water into that container, after a time of continuous pouring, the dirt gradually leaves and the clean replaces it. Ephesians 5:26 refer to the Word of God as the water that cleanse and sanctifies us, the containers. So continue to pour the Word of God in and watch, it has the power to deliver you. It is also important that we allow the word to be poured in by those whom the Lord has placed over us to shepherd us.

HAVING GOOD SUCCESS THROUGH THE WORD

This book of the law shall not depart out of thy mouth;
but thou shall meditate therein day and night,
that thou mayst observe to do according
to all that is written therein:
for then thou shalt make thy way prosperous,
and then thou shalt have good success.
Joshua 1:8 (KJV)

There are times when you will hear someone say, "I have been meditating on the Word of God, but I have not seen the success that the word promises." I must say that unfortunately, many of us have been taught wrong. We tend to see success as lots of money, big homes, and multiple luxurious cars, etc. and while those may be a result of success at times, having those things does not always mean that the person is successful. For many years that was the way I thought about success and because of that, I missed out on the opportunity to truly succeed.

Many have given up and others are heartsick because they believe that meditating on the word does not really work. The truth is, if we have all those things and are not in the will of God for our lives, then we are not successful at all. We can take a quick glance at Hollywood and see that while the finer things in life are great, those things do not fulfill many of them. Finding the will of God for your life and fulfilling it is true success. Yes, the blessing of God will flow when we are in the will of God, so continue to meditate on the Word of God and do what is written in it. Find yourself in the place of obedience to God's word and success will come in time.

Psalm 1:2 also tells us that when we meditate on the Word of God day and night, we will be like a tree that brings forth fruit in it is season. So know that you have a season in which you will see the fruits of you meditating on the Word of God. When all else fails, you can rely on the Word of God to take you from glory to glory and from strength to strength.

WATCH WHAT WE SAY

The level of life that we are experiencing now are the results of words that we have or have not been saying / speaking. Mark 11:23 Jesus says, "Truly I tell you, if anyone SAYS to this mountain, Go, throw yourself in the sea; and does not doubt in their heart, but believes that what they SAY will happen, it will be done for them." The word, 'say' in Hebrew translates *Amar* meaning to command, to tell, to give orders, or to declare. What Jesus is indicating to us is that when we open our mouths with the right words, we are changing situations and things around us.

For example, when we give a command it is an authoritative order. Usually, when someone in authority gives an order, it is carried out right away without questions. So it is when we use the right words, (the Word of God) we are literally giving directions and instructions that will be followed because we speak based on the authority of God's word. It is important for us to remember that when we are speaking God's word in faith, Angels are moving on our behalf. Psalm 103:20 (KJV) says, "Bless the LORD, ye His angels, that excel in strength, that do His commands, hearkening unto the voice of His word."

Another word that comes under the word command is *decree*. The Word of God says that when you decree a thing, it shall be established for you (see Job 22:28 NASB). Our words have power. In the same way that God spoke things into existence, He has also given us the ability to speak His word and see things change. How do we know this? Because we were created in His image and likeness. (See Gen. 1, Ps 105:31, Ps 107:25) Therefore we should use the word of God to give orders concerning our lives, our health, our homes, our children future, our finances, and everything else that concerns us.

Even where our protection is concerned, we must use the Word. Psalm 91:2 says, "I WILL SAY of the Lord, God you are my place of safety and protection. You are my God, and I trust you." Sometimes it may seem as if we are saying the right things and nothing is happening, but just continue to trust God. Say it until you see it.

At times we give up too quickly, because it looks like nothing is happening. We also use our own words to declare that nothing is happening and we believed it and that is why we end up seeing nothing sometimes. Other times we say it, but do not truly believe what we say. There is no shame to this game, because If you say something long enough, you will eventually believe it!

The word of God says that faith comes by hearing and hearing the word of God. (Romans 10:17) One of the ways that we were taught to have faith was to meditate on the word of God. One of the ways that we meditate is to say the word over and over again until it gets into your spirits. Once that word is in our spirits and we speak it, we will see it; even if we have to wait for a while. So again, no matter how long it takes, do not give up continue to use the word. It will bring about change.

Please let me share this last story with you. When I was in Bible school in Georgia, one of the classes I did was on the subject of Faith. We had an amazing instructor and she did an excellent job with the class. Of course, I had just learned ways in which we as believers feed and exercised our faith according to Mark 11:23-24 and decided that I would put to work what I had learned. I began to meditate on the word, confessed it, and muttered over it, among other things. Let me say that I was reignited! I had strength like an ox! I was smiling more and the joy of the Lord really showed up and overtook me. I had the favor of the Lord, money was coming in the mail, and I knew for sure I want to make everybody around me share in what I was experiencing.

After the course had ended, one Sunday morning as I was leaving the Sanctuary and walking to my car, I saw the Professor. She was standing along with about four or five of her colleagues (who were all ministers) having a conversation. I was so excited to see her, because I wanted to thanked her for the amazing job that she did in teaching the Word so effectively. I walked up to her and slapped my chest then I slapped her chest, bowed and jumbled everything that I was feeling in maybe one long sentence before her and her colleagues. After I stopped, the place went silent and all I heard the professor said was, "Gee Denva, did my class do all of that to you?" Wow! I was deflated. All I wanted to convey to the professor was, 'Woman of God, from my heart to yours, thank you! I have put into practice what you have taught me and it really worked.' Unfortunately that did not really turn out right. The point that I am making here, is that the word will work if we work it!

Another word for SAY is to *declare*. One word that defines declare is to *recount*. Psalm 2:7 states, "I will declare the Lord's decree: He said to me, You are my son; today I have become your father." Therefore, to declare the Lord's decree is to SAY what God has said to you based on His word. It could also mean to look at what He has done in the past on behalf of someone else and know that He will do the same for you. For example, God delivered Israel from Egyptian bondage. Therefore, we can stand and recount what He did for Israel and make declarations that He will do the same for us too.

It is said that Jewish fathers were instructed to teach their children to recount the miracles and mighty deeds of God, their deliver. Why? So that God's greatness will be known throughout the generations. It is easier to declare something when we know that God has made a promise or when there is a track record of it being done before. We know God's word works. We have seen it work in our lives before, we have heard of it working for others. Therefore it is easier to proclaim His mighty acts to others and declare that He will do the same for us when it is needed. (See Psalm 78:4; 145:4-12)

PRAYER

Lord God, I thank You for Your word that is a lamp to my feet and a light to my path. Help me to see the true value of Your word and to use it always because it is the final authority. I thank You that as I use Your word, You give to me wisdom, understanding and revelation. Your word changes my life and the lives of the people around me. Help me to confess Your word, pray Your word and declare Your word daily. Refresh my passion for You and Your word. Give me an unusual hunger for Your word.

In Jesus' name, amen.

NOTES

As you have experienced the power of God moving you from a place of brokenness to total freedom, what is that one thing that you believe that God has brought you to this earth to fulfill? If you do not know what your purpose is, pray and ask God to reveal it to you, then ask Him for the grace to start moving forward in it.

_____

_____

_____

_____

_____

_____

_____

_____

_____

_____

_____

_____

_____

_____

NOTES

NOTES

PART III

CHAPTER 17
Letters from the Lord

Sometimes when we are going through tough times or dealing with hard issues, an encouraging word is all we need to get us back on track. Countless times when I have taken up encouraging material to read, it is as if the Lord Himself speaks to me from the pages. With this outcome in mind, I pray that as you read these letters on the following pages, the right one will minister to you and you will hear the Spirit of God speaking to you. Different letters will minister to you at different times. It all depends on what your unique situations are. Also, the scriptures are made available so you can go back and recount them for yourself.

God is not wanting to condemn or beat anyone of us over the head. Instead, you will see that regardless of what the heading looks like, He has great encouragement to push you forward.

Encouraging letters on pages 100–114.

I AM WITH YOU

Daughter,

At times you may be tempted to feel like you are doing everything by yourself, but it is not so. Be comforted for I am with you. I never leave you to labor alone. Come, find rest in my presence. In my presence there is joy to it's fullest capacity and you will gain the strength that you need to carry out your daily duties. Daughter, I have seen your tears and I have heard your cries, but know that I am your helper and the provider for all that you need. Trust me! Put all into my hand. Look to me. Draw closer to me, I am your present help. Men may fail, systems may fail, but I, your loving Father, never fails. Your help comes from me.

I love you, daughter!

Scriptures:
Psalms 46:1; 65:4; 147:3

Isaiah 41:10; 45; 22

James 4:8

I HAVE PLANS FOR YOU

My daughter,

Why don't you stop running from what must be? My plans for you were from before the foundation of the world. Please remember that I know all about you, for I am with you always. I know your shortcomings and I know your strengths. You say you cannot speak, but I will speak through you. Allow me to show my glory through you daughter. If I wanted a perfect person to carry out my task, I would have created one. Look at my servants of old, they were not perfect, but I have used them greatly. Look to me. Come to me. I am the one that gives rest, I am the one who gives peace. Daughter, I am calling. I have great plans for your life. Come to me. I, your Father in Heaven, have need of you!

Your father

Scriptures:
Jeremiah 1:6,7
Matthew 11:28
John 14:27
Ephesians 1:7

I SEE YOU TRYING

Beloved Daughter,

Many times you find yourself wondering if you are in my will or if you are doing the right thing. I say yes, and I am with you.

Daughter, the fact that you start to do what you believe I told you to is proof that you love and trust me. Do not worry about what you are not, instead know who you are in me. Always keep in mind that it is not how you start, but how you finish that matters. For you see, the winner of the race is neither the swiftest nor the strongest, but it is the one who makes it to the end.

My daughter, continue in the race. Do not look at the small start. Though your beginnings are small, yet shall your latter end be greatly increased. Know that I have set you apart as my deliverer. Continue to walk in it!

I love you!

Dad

Scriptures:
Ecclesiastes 9:11
Isaiah 41:10
Zach 4:10
1Corinthians 15:58
Hebrew 12:1

WALLS OF PAIN

My Beloved Daughter,

You have asked where I was when you were being attacked, beaten and abandoned.

It was not my will that you go through what you went through, but the work of wicked men. You see daughter? They say in their hearts, "God does not see this," but I see it all. Vengeance is mine, and I will repay!

Daughter, I protected you from what could have been and I am still with you to deliver you. I have never left you, nor will I ever forsake you.

Daughter, I have seen your pain and I have seen the walls. Please allow me to take those walls down and heal you. I know the plans I have for you and my plans are not to harm you. My plans will give you the end you are looking for.

I love you daughter!

Scriptures:
Exodus 14: 13
2Choronicles 20:17
Isaiah 41:10-13
Jeremiah 29:11
Romans 12:19
Hebrew 10:30

A ROSE AMONG THORNS

My precious daughter,

The day you walked down the aisle, I was there with you. The joy you felt was because I was there. The commitment you made was sincere, but covenants are broken because of the sickness of the humans heart. Keep in mind that nothing comes to you unless it has passed through my loving hand.

My daughter, never mind how others judge you, I see you as a beautiful rose in the midst of thorns. Although you could not understand it then, the thorns were meant to protect you, not to destroy you.

I have removed from you those who would detour you from my eternal purpose. Do not see it as rejection or abandonment; instead, see it as my divine direction. Many are the plans of a man, but it is my plans that prevail. Daughter, the plans that I have for you are far greater than you can imagine and my plans always prevail. Rest in me, I will deliver you. Hold your head up and look to me, I am the lover of your soul.

Your protective Dad!

Scriptures:
Proverbs 19:21
Jeremiah 29:11

A HEART LIKE MINE

My daughter,

You love much and that is how I intended it. You give much and you always give your best. No wonder, you have a heart like mine. I love, so I gave. I gave my only Son. What costly gift!

Daughter, I have seen your pain even when no one else sees it. I have heard the cry of your heart when no one else hears it and I am healing you even now. Daughter, be of good cheer. Your share in this life will be pleasant, your part will be beautiful. So daughter, find my presence. It is the place where you get your confidence and your fill of joy

I am the lover of your soul,

Dad!

Scriptures:
Luke 6:38
John 3:16
Psalms 16

YOU ARE MY SERVANT

My dear servant,

Why do you believe that you are not called? I have said in my word that many are called but few are chosen. The few that are chosen are the ones that have answered the call. Have I not said to you over and over again that, "you are my witness in the earth that I am God?" Daughter, have you not realized by now that from before the foundation of the world I have prepared a work for you? You say you are not trained, you are not ready, but I have made you ready. Rise up! Now is the time to begin walking in my plan. Many are waiting for you. Say yes to my will. Tell yourself, "Not my will, but yours be done." Thank you, Daughter. Now begin walking!

You make me proud,

Dad

Scriptures:
Isaiah 45:5; 43:10; 42:6
Matthew 28:18; 22:14
Eph 2:10

WHY THE LONG STRUGGLE?

You say, "God, when will my breakthrough come? What am I doing wrong here? Is this a generational curse? Or did I disobey you? Okay Father, I repent!"

My daughter, I find you comical at times and just in case you are wondering, yes, you do put a smile on my face. Do not believe that I am punishing you for some seemingly sinful thing that you have done against me. Remember, I gave my Son for you while you were yet a sinner, so know that I love you with an everlasting love. Trust my judgment, daughter. I know what I am doing, I know what you have need of even before you ask. Know that I am working a far greater work on your behalf.

At the end of this you will come to me and say, "Abba, you have tested me. You have refined me like silver. You laid burdens on my back. You let people ride over my head. You took me through the fire and the water, but now you have brought me into a place of abundance." Yes daughter, be patient! You are at the cusp of that place of abundance.

I can be trusted,

Dad!

Scriptures:
Psalms 66:10
Jeremiah 29:11
MSG 31:3
Matthew 6:8
Romans 5:8

WE HAVE WORK TO DO

My daughter,

You make me proud in so many ways. I have especially enjoyed the times you spend with me in prayer. Daughter, the future I have planned for you is great. It is always my pleasure to exceed your expectations. Remember, daughter, I am able to do exceedingly above all that you ask or think.

One thing though, surrender the pain of your past to me. Turn your anger over to me and let me heal you. Remember, the agony my Son went through on the cross was to give you the healing and the peace that you so desire. Trust me with your pain, daughter. I am your healer. Know that we have work to do!

Dad!

Scriptures:
Exodus 15:26
Isaiah 53:5
1Corinthians 3:9
Eph 3:20

WHY DO YOU LOOK BACK?

My little one,

You started out well, but why are you now looking back? Did you not remember that the race is not given to the swift nor the strong, but to the one who endures to the end? My daughter, endure hardship like a good soldier and know that if you do not faint or look back, you will receive the prize. Quiet your heart, daughter, and listen to for my instructions. I have a grandiose path ahead of you. Continue to go forward. I am with you!

Dad

Scriptures:
Eccl 9:11
Galatians 5:11
2 Timothy 2:3-4

THE GREAT PRETENDER

My daughter,

When I call you the great pretender, I am not trying to insult you. I am merely telling you to be the you that I have called you to be. Do you realize that there is not another like you on the planet? You are fearfully and wonderfully made. Daughter, in the midst of pretending, the authentic anointing to be and to do is laying dormant in you. Do you realize that I have called you to greatness? Yes, I have! Spend time with me and let me show you the real you. You will be surprised when the real you is discovered!

Your loving Dad!

Scriptures:
Psalms 139

OFFENDED ONE

Daughter,

Did I not tell you that offense would come, but woe to that one who brings it? Do not look at your sisters and brothers as the offender, but see who is behind them pulling the strings. It is our enemy, the Devil.

Daughter, I expect you to walk in my love because this is the true mark of my children. Remember my word, "If you say you love me who you do not see, and hate your brothers and sisters whom you see, then you do not walk in the truth." Now rise up from where you are and forgive. You cannot move forward while holding on to the past. So let go of the past and move forward. I am with you.

Your all seeing Dad!

Scriptures:
Matthew 6:14
Luke 17:1 NIV
Philippians 3:13
1John 4:20

ASK BIG! THINK BIG!

My beloved daughter,

How is it that you believe me to help others but doubt when it comes to you? Do you not understand that I love you too? I am the good shepherd who loves and cares for every sheep. If one strays, I will leave the ninety-nine and go look for the one.

Learn my ways, daughter. I do not make a promise and go back on my word. Trust me in all things! It gives me great pleasure when my children believes me for great things. Ask me to do the exceedingly, abundantly, above all that you ask or think. Ask big! Think big! I am a big God and I will do big things for you!

I love you,

Father

Scriptures:
Psalm 125:1
John 10:11
2Corinthians 1:20
Ephesians 3:20

RESTORATION IS IN PROGRESS

My daughter,

The process of restoring may not look and feel good to you right now. In the process of restoration, I have to first strip and clean away the old before you see the visible progress. I have started the process of restoration in you, so sit tight and wait in expectance for the finished work to unfold.

I am your Father and I am the one who is doing the work. Know that you will not be harmed or destroyed in this process. I only do what is best for you.

Do not be dismayed over what you have lost for I Am restoring the years, your health, your prosperity, your family, your joy, and your peace. Rejoice daughter. I am working on your behalf.

Know that I love you,

Dad

Scriptures:
Isaiah 43:19
Joel 2:25

I SEE YOUR HEART DAUGHTER

Daughter,

I see you have a heart to bring me glory and that you will do. Just the mere fact that you want what I want for you, brings me glory.

You have asked that I make your heart a highway for my presence and that I have done. Wherever you go, know that you are carrying my presence.

Daughter do not be so hard on yourself, none of this is done with the mind, it is the working of my Spirit. So remember daughter, it is not by might, nor by power, but by my spirit. Know that I love you and have great plans for you.

Your faithful Dad!

Scriptures:
Isaiah 40:3
Exodus 33:14
Zechariah 4:6

PRAYER FOR SALVATION

Speaking of moving forward, the most important move that anyone of us can and should make is one from darkness into the marvelous light of Jesus Christ. Without this first move, one would have been moving around in Darkness and not forward.

You ask, "How do I accept Christ in my heart?", the Bible declares,

*If you will confess with your mouth the Lord Jesus,
and believe in your heart that God has raised Him
from the dead, you shall be saved. For with the heart
man believes unto righteousness; and with the mouth
confession is made unto salvation.*

Rom 10:9-10

I encourage you to make Jesus Christ the Lord and Savior of your life today by praying this simple, but powerful prayer. Mean it from the depths of your heart and you will be saved.

Let us pray a prayer of salvation:

*Lord Jesus, I believe that you are the Son of God.
I believe that You went to the cross and You died for my
sins. I believe that You rose from the dead and You are
seated at the right hand of the Father. I ask you now to
come into my heart. Forgive me of all my sins. Wash me
in Your blood and cleanse me from all unrighteousness.
Be my Lord, and live Your life through me.
I confess right now that I am saved, amen.*

NOTES

Hopefully by now you have experienced some deliverance. You have also made up your mind to move foward in God, doing what He has ordained for you to do (in God's timing, of course). Every now and then God will use one of those letters in section three to encourage you and to push you forward so that you can continue in the faith. Take time to make your own notes of what the Spirit of God is saying to you.

God bless you.

_____

_____

_____

_____

_____

_____

_____

_____

_____

_____

_____

_____

_____

_____

_____

_____

_____

NOTES

NOTES

References

All Scripture verses, unless otherwise indicated, are taken from THE HOLY BIBLE, NEW INTERNATIONAL VERSION®, NIV® Copyright © 1973, 1978, 1984, 2011 by Biblica, Inc.® Used by permission. All rights reserved worldwide.

Scripture taken from the New King James Version®. Copyright © 1982 by Thomas Nelson. Used by permission. All rights reserved.

The Holy Bible, King James Version. Cambridge Edition: 1769; King James Bible Online, 2015. <http://www.kingjamesbibleonline.org/>

Amar—The Hebrew–Greek Study Bible, KJV. Revised edition by AMG International, Inc., 1991.

Scripture taken from the Modern English Version. Copyright © 2014 by Military Bible Association. Used by permission. All rights reserved.

Scripture quotations are taken from the Holy Bible, New Living Translation, copyright ©1996, 2004, 2007 by Tyndale House Foundation. Used by permission of Tyndale House Publishers, Inc., Carol Stream, Illinois 60188. All rights reserved.

Clinton, Tim, Archibald Hart, and George Ohlschlager, *Caring For People God's Way*. Personal and Emotional issues, Addictions, Grief, and Trauma. Nashville, TN: Thomas Nelson, Inc., 2005.

Eckhardt, John, *Prayers That Rout Demons*. Lake Mary, FL: Charisma House, A Strong Company, 2008.

McGolerick, Elizabeth Weiss, *The Father Daughter Relationship*, posted October 11, 2012 <www.sheknows.com/>. *Fatherhood-Philosophy for Everyone: The Dao of Daddy*, edited by Michael W. Austin. <www.shrines.com/parenting>.

Russel, A. J., *God Calling*. Uhrichsville, Ohio: Barbour Publishing, Inc., 1989.

Dictionary.com. Retrieved February 23, 2015, from Dictionary.com website: <http://dictionary.reference.com/browse/comfort?s=t>

Merriam-Webster.com. Retrieved February 23, 2015, from Merriam-Webster.com website: <http://www.merriam-webster.com/dictionary/compassion>

Wikipedia.com. Retrieved February 23, 2015, from Wikipedia.com website: <http://en.wikipedia.org/wiki/Compassion>

www.ingramcontent.com/pod-product-compliance
Lightning Source LLC
Chambersburg PA
CBHW061956040426
42447CB00010B/1778